#ENTRY LEVEL BOSS

To the 24-year-old girl who was utterly convinced that her career was already a lost cause. Look at us, honey. Look at what we did.

Love,
Older You

HOW TO GET
ANY JOB YOU WANT

#ENTRY LEVEL BOSS

ALEXA SHOEN

HARPER
BUSINESS

An Imprint of HarperCollins Publishers

First published in 2020 by Scribe Publications, Australia

This edition published by arrangement with Scribe Publications, for sale
throughout South Asia

First published in India in 2020 by Harper Business
An imprint of HarperCollins *Publishers*
A-75, Sector 57, Noida, Uttar Pradesh 201301, India
www.harpercollins.co.in

2 4 6 8 10 9 7 5 3 1

P-ISBN: 978-93-5357-961-6
E-ISBN: 978-93-5357-962-3

Printed and bound at
Thomson Press (India) Ltd

Contents

Preface

What I remember most about the job search is the locked doors.

You see, when I was twenty, I became obsessed with landing an internship. I used to lock myself in my university bedroom on weeknights and click through jobs listings for hours.

And I do mean *hours*. I still have relatively organised folders sitting in my inbox that can prove to you how hard I was trying. (I fished a boatload of embarrassing emails out of those folders for this book.)

If you put up an internship posting online any time between 2009 and 2012, chances are I considered applying.

I had lists. One time, I found the mother lode of lists. A clever internet search landed me an alphabetised directory of every advertising agency in Chicago. (I also found the same list for London.)

I spent days with that list. I probably still have it saved somewhere, in one of those relatively organised folders. Over the course of hours, I bookmarked all 400+ websites and copied down every email address I could find. I felt the adrenaline rush of a job well done.

I'd close my laptop and get ready for bed.

It would cross my mind, maybe while I was brushing my teeth, that I hadn't actually accomplished anything, aside from copying and pasting links, adding to a never-ending list of hot prospects to check out tomorrow.

But that thought would leave as quickly as it came. I'd worked all night on this. I was going to be so very, very employed. Any day now.

Yep, just … any day now.

Any.

Day.

Now.

This book is for everybody who's ever felt that way.

How to use this book

The sole purpose of this book is to elegantly guide you from Point A to Point B:

Freak-Out Mode → *Interviews for Jobs You'll Genuinely Enjoy*

The 9-step approach laid out on the following pages has been adapted from the course curriculum that I developed for #ENTRYLEVELBOSS School (#ELB School for short!), a boot camp designed to rein in the chaos of the job search. A fitness plan for becoming gainfully employed, if you will. Which means I'm like Joe Wicks, or Oprah, or Kanye, or something — but for CVs.

I'm proud to tell you that we've been successfully transforming panicking job seekers into hired-and-happy humans since 2017, in fields ranging from public relations and sales to social work and environmental law. Over the years, I have guided thousands of students through the #ENTRYLEVELBOSS job search approach. I receive messages every single week from ex-students who, on their first day on the job, write to me from their new employee email addresses. I love those emails, but if I'm honest with you, I love the messages from the people who *haven't* been hired yet even more. 'It's weird to feel this excited about trying to find a job,' someone wrote to me once. 'I don't know how you manage to do it, but you somehow made job searching … fun.' (She sent me an email just three weeks later telling me that she had landed exactly the kind of job she was hoping to get.)

Cheerful messages from people who haven't even got the job yet, can you imagine? It's a pretty cool magic trick, I think, to score a job you genuinely enjoy without overwhelm or despair. I'd like to help you do that, too.

How to get the most out of this book

I wrote this book knowing that you'd want to be shady and read the entire thing through without doing any homework first. Go ahead, binge read! Understand why your current approach isn't getting you the right results. Take a tour of your fancy new strategy, front to back, and digest the reasoning. Underline stuff as you go.

Then, come back to the task lists at the end of each section. Flip back through when you want to recall how I phrased something or remind yourself why I warned you to do X instead of Y. Take everything in and then put it to work at a pace that feels right for you.

Your #ENTRYLEVELBOSS packing list

- Internet access
- A professional email address (use your full name instead of OneAchingHeart4433)
- A way to stay organised (go to **entrylevelboss.com/dayone** for digital suggestions)

And, finally, my one promise to you

You will never again find yourself at a dead end, panicking without a plan.

There are lots of dangers to navigate throughout the course of any job search: internal panic, a lack of confidence, existential dread, bad communication habits, uncontrollable external factors, hiring managers, the annoying human needs of said hiring managers (see: weekends, sleep, etc.). The real reason that any job search spins out of control, though, is not because of these things. It is because, when faced with any combination of these demons, you get stuck. Everything feels out of your control. You don't see a next move in front of you.

If you use this system, you will always be able to unstick yourself. This is my promise to you.

Look: you are not going to be magically employed by the end of the week just because you happened to pick this book up off the shelf. You'll quickly learn that I wouldn't lie to you like that. But if you try it my way, you will be able to put one foot in front of the other, to twist out of handcuffs, to walk through walls. You will be that person who always has another trick up their sleeve. Whatever it takes — within reason — until you arrive at your final destination and see that first paycheque in your bank account.

Until you're hired and happy.

Meet me, the person who wrote this book

In 1999, a truly terrible film was released in cinemas. *Baby Geniuses* achieved an impressively low 2% rating on Rotten Tomatoes. The basic premise is that babies are — you guessed it — legitimate Einstein-level geniuses from birth right up until the moment they learn to communicate in spoken human language. As soon as they learn to speak, they forget everything. They become fallible humans. All their baby genius knowledge is lost.

This film has become the metaphor I turn to when I am asked about this book.

I spent the first half of my twenties in education, unemployed, or underemployed — and job searching the entire time. I spent the second half being sought after by cool companies and growing my career at a breakneck speed. Once I crossed that magical threshold, it felt like I had entered into another realm. I finally understood what pretentious people were talking about when they would casually say, 'The best time to get a job is when you already have one, eh? I haven't sent anyone a CV in years, but I feel like I'm always turning down offers, haha!'

As soon as that transition happened — they wanted ME, finally! — I made a decision. On top of building my own career, I also started documenting my successes (and my missteps) as they were happening. I wanted to acquire as much knowledge as possible about career growth, so that I could pass it back to all the people who were still in education, unemployed, or underemployed. Like sending buckets of water down the line to throw on a raging fire.

I felt a sense of urgency. I had to tell people how this job search thing worked. I wanted to equip them with the tools they needed to survive out there. I wanted to teach them how they could become one of the lucky ones. Because — this chosen group of people? It wasn't that they were all Oxbridge grads or working for their parents' companies, it was that they had — consciously or because of dumb luck — figured out how to play the game.

I had to get the word out before I forgot. I had to do it now, before I became too much of a grown-up, before I became too employable, frankly, and forgot what it was like. Because I could see, so clearly, just how many of these elite, fancy, cool, job-having grown-ups had forgotten — just like the plotline of *Baby Geniuses*.

Those grown-ups were the reason I became a career coach at 25. Throughout my early career — a repeated smattering of hard-won contractor stints, hourly internships, and six-week freelance projects — the grown-ups consistently let me down whenever the topic of recruitment came up. I'd watch them tear apart CVs for sport. 'Oh my God, look at what this one said on theirs. So stupid! Ugh, trying to find people for these jobs is so exhausting and boring,' they'd lament to each other. I heard the same thing said a thousand different ways, over and over. They were *making fun of us*.

Sitting in their offices, lucky enough to be half-employed for a few weeks at a time, my blood boiled on behalf of every job seeker in the world. We: the unlucky, the unemployed, the underemployed. The bright-eyed dreamers, the hopefuls, the ones trying to break into a new industry, the young and the not-so-young, the ones who just want a more fulfilling job than the one we have right now. *Please help. We want to come work for you. Why don't you want us back?*

It was heartbreaking and eye-opening to find annoyance instead of empathy again and again. It was a situation I felt so emotionally connected to — trying to find work and getting shut out time after time without understanding why. What a privilege it must be to poke fun at the people who are applying to be your assistants, your colleagues, your collaborators. I was taken aback by the total amnesia of the grown-ups. How could they forget? What a luxury, I thought, to forget.

Even though I was young, I understood that it could go one of two ways:

1. *The hiring managers could take an extra five freaking seconds per application and stop writing people off for the wrong reasons.* They could try to see through what they perceived to be the rough-around-the-edges parts, and chalk up any errors to this person just not knowing any better. Did a poorly formatted CV really mean this candidate wouldn't be helpful in the office? I felt convinced that the person they were looking for was somewhere in their inbox, if these hiring managers would just take the time to put themselves in someone else's shoes. But that was unlikely, so …

2. *Someone else needed to find a way to help all these people.* All these applicants — no matter how experienced — shared the same problem. They were terrible at explaining themselves, but it was only because they didn't seem to know how. From where I was sitting, it looked like a communication issue more than anything else. A CV and cover letter are just words, at the end of the day. And I knew I was a *great* writer, so I figured: it might as well be me.

I get asked a lot if the advice in this book is only applicable to young people who are just starting their careers. My answer is no. Because my original audience was young, I managed to develop an insanely effective job search approach that works *even* if you have zero experience, *even* if you have zero knowledge of office politics, *even* if you have never had a single job in your life, *even* if you're convinced you're the least hireable person on the planet. I set out to develop a plan that would work when you had absolutely nothing to bring to the table yet. So imagine my surprise when I started to realise what this approach could do for job seekers who had a few things going for them already. (And PS: I find that most people — yes, even recent school leavers or university graduates — have more to bring to the table than they think.)

I am absolutely the type of person who, by this point, would have googled the author of this book. I'd be all, 'Alright, nice person with the ideas, who are you?'

If you've done the same, I'm sure you found my websites, my Spotify, some very old YouTube videos, my various social media accounts, who knows what else. Maybe I will have gone viral and become a controversial public figure in-between me finishing this manuscript and you reading it. Either way, here's some additional colour that you won't be able to find out about me anywhere else:

If a speaker asks for questions at the end of a panel, I will always come up with one on the spot because I get too sad for them if nobody else in the audience has one.

If you put on 'I Want You Back' by The Jackson 5, I will scream

*every word at the top of my lungs no matter what time of day it is —
a habit that got me in trouble occasionally at university parties that
were trying to stay under the radar.*

I'm more of a nature person than I had previously thought.

*My least favourite foods are anchovies and sardines, because the
idea of a fish I can smoosh with a spoon stresses me out.*

*I fantasise about growing up to be a morning person. In said
fantasies, that fictitious fully-grown-adult version of me will also
own a cake stand. The kind with a clear glass lid so that you can see
how much cake is left.*

As for my *professional* history …

The irony is not lost on me that, in writing a book about the
job search process, I have no idea where to start in explaining how
I know all the things I know and why you should follow my advice.
Several times while attempting to write this section, I have freaked
out about my own CV: *Is it cool enough? Relatable enough? Will it
make sense to people who just randomly stumble across this book
on a shelf? Am I the right person? Should we have all waited for
someone else to write this book instead? How can I prove to you that
I know what I'm talking about?*

Funny, isn't it, how we so easily trip over our own personal
narratives when we could craft somebody else's elevator pitch in a
heartbeat.

Anyway, hi, I'm Alexa: global career coach extraordinaire and
creator of the #ENTRYLEVELBOSS job search approach. I transform panicking job seekers into hired-and-happy professionals.

I did not study employment in any academic sense. I've never
worked as a recruiter. I'm just somebody who graduated at the tail
end of a recession, inelegantly struggled to start my own career,
and then became curious about why the job search felt like such
an uphill battle. I've been deeply obsessed with the topic ever since,
and have now ushered thousands of #ENTRYLEVELBOSS students

successfully into employment using the 9-step approach I created based on years of trial and error, conversation, curiosity, and study.

But if I could offer up a single qualification for why you should trust me, it's simply that I spent the first several years of my career applying for a lot of jobs I never got, and through that heart-wrenching and nausea-inducing process, I figured out a few tricks. And I wrote them down. That's my big pitch.

I started sending out the #ENTRYLEVELBOSS newsletter — in which I documented crucial things I was learning about becoming a professional adult, such as how to apologise for being 15 minutes late for your final-round interview — when I was just beginning my own career.

I'd graduated from university four years earlier, but I was only two and a half years into being a fully grown professional human once you factored in my straight-outta-undergrad Master's degree. At the time, it felt as if I'd haphazardly landed on my feet. I was an accidental freelance copywriter, and I finally had *almost* enough work to feel emotionally and financially safe enough to stop looking for a Real Salaried Full-Time Job. At least for a while. Which was great news, because, by my calculation, I'd been steadily looking for work for five years.

I genuinely enjoyed my profession, but, come on, it wasn't like I'd planned for any of it to happen. I had only started freelancing because I couldn't find a 'real' job. I had tried, I had applied, I had failed. Most of my applications simply sailed off into the dark beyond, to the Land of Misfit CVs perhaps, never to be heard from again. As for the employers that did want me, they didn't ever seem to want me full-time. An hourly internship that might become a paid position? I took it. A six-month contract that might be extended, but we can't promise you anything? I took it. Ten hours a week, on a month-to-month basis? I took it. A thousand emails left unanswered. A thousand false starts. A thousand rejections. I can craft a mighty strategic narrative around this story now, one that shines a light on all the things I learned during the journey, but when it was my reality, it felt like I was running a marathon I hadn't signed up for, attempting to cross a finish line that never seemed to appear on the horizon.

During my last year of university, I'd watched what felt like all of my classmates get hired into massive corporations to become accountants and analysts and junior executives. They hadn't seemed smarter than me when we were all drinking cheap beer and studying in the same library, but maybe they were. Maybe I just hadn't noticed. *I should have studied accounting. All the accountants have jobs now.*

For a long time, I felt a lot of shame about never finding that first official foothold on the ladder. Even after I'd built a successful career as one of the most sought-after freelancers in the European startup world, I kept looking for what I could've sworn I had been promised: a full-time job with benefits and annual leave and an office coffee machine. All I wanted, so badly, for years, was to hear someone say, 'You! Yes, you! I see the talent, and I need you FULL-TIME! Grab your coat and get over here, you're officially on payroll, kid. This is your happy ending. This is your life now.'

I wanted this so much that, even after I got it, I continued to build an entire company around making that dream come true for others. Because I believe that everybody deserves their shot at landing a job they genuinely like. Because I believe that looking for work should be more celebrated, more straightforward, and more fun. And because I believe that a great permanent job, the kind where you're getting paid to spend your days solving the problems you really want to solve, is one of the worthiest pursuits in the world.

The whole story

Throughout this book, I'll be sharing emails and cover letters and CVs from my past, most of which are entirely unedited and unredacted. Because of my start-and-stop freelancing career — plus the fact that I've lived in multiple countries — I thought you might find it helpful to have a CliffsNotes version of my life history to date. In case you're feeling nosy. Now, in order to lay this out for you, I'm going to do something you're never supposed to do on CVs. I'm going to start at the beginning. (There, take it, your first lesson: Do as I say, not as I do.)

FULL-TIME KID, N/A

San Diego, CA, and Las Vegas, NV | 1989–2007

A happy childhood. I have two parents and a younger brother. When I was 14, we finally got a dog and we named her Rizzo — a multi-purpose reference to both Grease *and* The Muppets. *She was bilingual and knew the days of the week.*

UNIVERSITY STUDENT (ENGLISH MAJOR), UNIVERSITY OF NOTRE DAME

South Bend, IN | 2007–2011

I don't think I've wanted anything in my life as badly as I wanted to go to Notre Dame. I didn't really have the scores for it, but I refused to come up with a Plan B. I'll talk more about this later and show you an email I wrote when I was 17 years old.

GIRL WHO STUDIES ABROAD, EUROPE

Barcelona, Spain | Summer 2009

I spent the summer between my second and third years of university alone in Barcelona, learning Spanish, and it turned my world upside down. I fell in love for the first time; I fell in love with the language, I fell in love with Europe. I take back what I just said — I wanted to live in Europe just as badly as I wanted to go to Notre Dame. I would go on to spend the next several years hustling my way into achieving that goal.

MASTER'S STUDENT (JAZZ VOCAL PERFORMANCE), LEEDS COLLEGE OF MUSIC

Leeds, United Kingdom | 2011–2013

The summer before my final year of university, I had a pretty drunken lunch with my mother that wound up with us, six hours later, seeing a seventies cover band in a local San Diego bar. I have always been a singer, and had an intense, drunken revelation in which I realised I needed to pursue music. I quickly sobered up and decided to make a more safe and respectable choice for my career — but, remember, I also wanted to live in Europe. So I attempted to kill a lot of birds with one stone and went straight from university to northern England to do a Master's in Jazz Vocal Performance. I still make music.

FIRST 'REAL' JOBS, MULTIPLE EMPLOYERS
San Francisco, CA | 2013–2014

I picked the first job that would offer me the slightest hope of making $40,000 a year after three initial months of internship work paid by the hour (which, by the way, I never completed). I hated that job. I sat in a windowless office. I had reverse culture shock from England, I didn't know many people in the city, I had situational depression that spiralled into very real depression. I might refer to San Francisco throughout the book as my Worst Year Ever because it absolutely was. The hatred I felt for my career and the panic I felt about my life during that dark period are, on the other hand, part of what inspired me to start writing once things got good.

PROFESSIONAL HUSTLER, SELF-EMPLOYED
Berlin, Germany | 2014–2016

In San Francisco, I became obsessed with finding a way to get back to Europe. I got let go from a contract on the same day my apartment lease ended, and I took it as a sign. I'd never even visited Berlin. I moved without a job, without a visa, without a partner, without a plan. The only two 'references' I knew that could even vouch for the city were a SoundCloud employee I'd befriended on LinkedIn during a previous job search stint, and a romantic fling who'd been recruited for a role in Berlin at one point — the second of whom offered me some very clever, very un-American advice: 'Go for six weeks,' he said. 'See if you like it.'

EXCEPTIONAL TALENT

London, United Kingdom | 2017

In Berlin, I ran my own consulting practice and rapidly transformed myself from entry-level talent into well-paid senior consultant for publicly traded technology companies. By following my curiosity, I became a specialist in an obscure-but-needed form of communication design work, helping software teams to build websites that would look good and function well in multiple languages simultaneously. I also started the #ENTRYLEVELBOSS newsletter.

Thanks to those two particularly niche CV high-lights, I was able to make the case that I was the best in the world at what I did. I decided to apply for a prestigious immigration route into the United Kingdom called the Tier 1 Exceptional Talent Visa. It's effectively a golden ticket. Just 200 are given out each year for people who work in technology.

CONTENT STRATEGIST, FACEBOOK

London, United Kingdom | 2017–2019

I knew I was really good at what I did, but part of me still craved the one thing I'd never had before: a 'real' full-time job, the kind with the benefits and the annual leave and the office coffee machine. I wanted to know what it was like.

There was another part of it, too. I'd been writing the #ENTRYLEVELBOSS email for more than two years and I was successfully teaching thousands of people how to get hired, but I'd never actually held a salaried position myself. I'd been freelance for my whole career.

Basically, I validated this entire method when I got an offer for a senior tech position at Facebook.

FOUNDER, #ENTRYLEVELBOSS

Worldwide | 2019–present

These days, I'm working full-time on all things #ENTRYLEVELBOSS. My goal is to empower job seekers like you to take your career destiny into your own hands. We are constantly teaching new students through #ELB School, the job search boot camp that inspired this book. Come check us out:

entrylevelboss.com/school

As far as how this book thing happened? Well, I continued sending out the #ENTRYLEVELBOSS email, even while employed at Facebook. I slowly put together a book proposal. Kind of like sending in an application for a dream job, just to see what would happen. Then, I quit my job to write a book about how to find a job. Look at that — wild.

I have had a very, very, very lucky life. I really want to acknowledge that.

I'm healthy, I'm white, I'm straight, I'm cisgendered, I'm able-bodied, I'm educated, I'm a native English speaker, I come from a loving family that could lend me money. I was born into the type of privilege that offered me the permission to dream up crazy things, like moving to Europe just because it felt good. I am overwhelmingly grateful for that.

I don't know what your situation was like. We might be twins separated at birth, but we probably aren't. I have a good relationship with my parents and I feel like they would have told me something like that by now.

There are social barriers and prejudices that many job seekers face that can make the search for work, well, a lot more hard work. The approach outlined in this book has been tried and tested by thousands of #ENTRYLEVELBOSS students, many of whom have financial backgrounds, family situations, or race and gender identities that are different to my own. Regardless, I want to acknowledge that there may be specific techniques that are easier for some readers to deploy than others. I want you to make your own calls in those moments, because you know your own situation better than I ever could. My aim is simply to tell you everything I know about how to get yourself hired as quickly as possible with the skills that you already have and in the situation that you are facing, today. Because I believe that what I'm teaching should be available to absolutely everyone, not just passed along haphazardly around certain kinds of dinner tables.

Earlier on, I told you that the only pitch I can really offer you is that I went through my own trial-and-error and I wrote it all down. Hopefully, somewhere in these pages, in amongst all my mistakes and learnings, you'll find something useful. Something that will act as a weapon for whatever unique version of the job search battle you might be fighting out there.

Part 1

We Gotta Talk About the Job Search

'In order to go fast, go slow.'

Somebody Wise

14 Incorrect beliefs about how employment works

At several hundred points over the course of my career, I have made poor decisions based on assumptions that I took as fact. We all have such strong opinions about employment, don't we? I over-hear them all the time: somebody ranting about how things work in an industry they've never worked in, somebody else moaning that they would never have a chance at getting a job they've yet to apply for, and so on, and so forth.

Because of how rapidly the world keeps changing on us — employment-wise and just in general, frankly — I try to identify and challenge my own assumptions whenever I can. Throughout this book, I'm often going to ask you do this, too. To start us off with a bang, I have assembled this list of 14 incorrect beliefs I used to hold about employment — and all the things I now know to be true instead.

Incorrect belief #1: *'I should cast the widest net possible with my job search so that I don't miss an opportunity.'*
Let me tell you about a situation I often run into with recent grad-uates, with school leavers, with experienced talent, with pretty much everybody:

Acquaintance: I'm looking for a marketing job!

Me: Nice. What sort of job are you looking for?

Acquaintance: Any sort of marketing position.
Or operations.

Me: Oh. Uhh, okay, so ... Paid social? Analytics or content?
Which industry?

Acquaintance: I want to work in marketing! Or maybe
management.

Me: *exits stage right*

'I want to work in marketing' gives me exactly nothing to go on. I cannot help you. Here's what's rolling around in my head during that kind of conversation: *Do you prefer B2B or B2C marketing? Do you have any experience with AdWords? Are you more interested in community management? If so, have you analysed organic engagement data before? What do you know about SEO? More specifically, what do you know about how code needs to be organised in order to implement SEO? Have you worked with a CMS before? How experienced are you with email marketing automation? Could you write the content, too? Do you know WordPress? Are you a good writer? How quickly could you create content? Could you write your own editorial calendar? Do you have contacts to journalists in any specific industry? Do you know what you're talking about?*

The instinct to be vague makes a ton of sense. You could be great at lots of things! You don't want to say anything that will get you crossed off the list before you've even had a chance to prove yourself. In Step 1, I am going to get up on my soapbox and give you my big speech on the powers of specialisation and how asking for exactly the kind of job you want will accelerate your career growth, not hinder it.

I know, I know. You don't want to get 'stuck' on the wrong path. To illustrate where we're headed, I can only offer real help to one of these two people:

Person 1: I'm looking for a job in marketing.

Person 2: I'm looking for an entry-level marketing role. I know that a lot of marketing is maths and data these days, which I think is really interesting. From different marketing job descriptions I've seen online, I think I would like SEO and SEM. Getting it right seems like a strategy game. I also read this interesting article about … is it called real-time bidding? I had no idea how those social media ads worked. It makes so much sense! I also think it would be really cool to work in an industry that I already know a little bit about, so I want to find a job that deals with sports somehow. Maybe a surfing brand?

With a few extra sentences, Person 2 is able to quickly explain that he or she actually knows what a marketing department really does. I know what industry interests this person. And, crucially, I have enough information to know whether or not I can help.

Incorrect belief #2: *'I don't want to pigeonhole myself into the wrong path before I know what I want.'*
Career paths don't follow straight lines anymore. That ladder you were supposed to climb has become a 4D monster, constantly shifting and decaying and moving and sprouting new heads. At the rate at which the global economy and technology are changing, you could not possibly predict where your career will take you. It's almost impossible to pigeonhole yourself, because the modern economy will ask you to keep adapting again and again. You get to want something today, and you get to want something else five years from now.

You've probably been on a hike, right? You know how you have to choose a route at the beginning, but then trails merge and separate, and sometimes you can jump from one trail to another? In order to ever get *anywhere*, whether that's to go on a Saturday morning hike or build a career, you have to choose a starting point. It doesn't have to be the obvious trail that goes straight up from the car park, but you have to start walking. Choose. Yes, it will change the course of your life. It may change the course of history, in fact. But just keep reminding yourself that you literally *cannot get anywhere* unless you start walking.

Incorrect belief #3: *'It's really hard to break into X industry.'*
I sometimes find that the best thing I can do as a career coach is to give you the permission you refuse to give yourself. So, here it goes:

We hold ourselves back from applying for the jobs we want. We hear that it's a 'tough industry to get into' and we don't bother trying. We don't even look into how to figure it out because we believe what we were told. We assume that we will fail. But here's the thing: hundreds of thousands of people are employed in all those dream jobs that someone deemed too unrealistic to chase after, and all those cool industries you are dying to work in are multi-billion-dollar behemoths that need a giant workforce. You are allowed to step up to the plate, if you like. No matter who you are. You are allowed to take your shot.

Do your research. Go see for yourself. Do not tell me how hard it is if you haven't tried.

Incorrect belief #4: *'I have to choose between an interesting job and a high-paying job.'*
I spent the early moments of my own career chasing not money, necessarily, but security. I thought that the big corporations would

be safe. I thought that people with analyst-type jobs were less likely to get fired. Armed with a boatload of assumptions based on who-knows-what, I made up all kinds of stories in my head about which career paths might be riskier than others. Importantly, I never bothered to actually ask anybody whether or not my assumptions were true.

Here's what I can tell you: there are some career paths where you get paid a lot of money right off the bat. There are some career paths where you make very little money for a long time, and then — if you stay the course — you can wind up making a ton of money. There are some career paths that we associate with prestige or a certain social class that actually make *less* money than we think they do. There are plenty of electricians, for example, who make more money than the office worker down the street. Moreover, there are factors beyond salary and passion that you will want to consider over the course of your career. The hours, the team, the benefits, the annual leave, the opportunity for growth, the on-site childcare, the flexibility to work from home, the team dynamics, the office snacks, and many more.

If you're convinced that you need to make a binary decision, you most likely just don't know what all your options are yet. I certainly don't. I'm a career coach, and there's no way I could write down a comprehensive list of every job that exists in the world, and I certainly couldn't guess the salary range for each of those positions.

Incorrect belief #5: *'I don't need to enjoy my job. Jobs are just supposed to be jobs.'*
Too many of us were taught that career fulfilment is an out-of-reach indulgence. A few lucky people might get to like their job, sure, but the rest of us are just meant to suffer, day in, day out. If this belief is present in your family or your marriage or your

community, I want you question it fiercely. You don't owe it to anybody else to suffer. You get to look for — at least *look* for — a career you will enjoy.

Listen, working a job you love is still hard work, but working a job you hate is so much harder. There are so many interesting puzzles to solve in this world. When you find a job solving the kind of puzzles that light you up, you will be amazed at how your outlook will change. My hope is for everyone to experience that feeling every day.

Before accepting, blindly, that your fate in life is to grin and bear it for the next 40 years, give yourself permission to do a little research about something — anything — that sparks your curiosity. Go and see what's out there. After all, unless you believe in reincarnation, you only get one life.

Incorrect belief #6: *'I am a university graduate. A nondescript job of some kind is being held for me out there somewhere because, like I said, I am a university graduate.'*
At least once a week, an email just like this one lands in my inbox:

Hi Alexa! I'm starting to get really frustrated about not finding a job that shows off my potential. I graduated with a first-class degree, and I won an award for the best undergraduate student of all time. I speak French. I'm a world-renowned macramé champion. I volunteer at Christmas. I am ready to start my career. What am I missing?

Congratulations on all your wonderful accomplishments. Genuinely. If this is you, I want to tell you that you've done an incredible job at taking advantage of all that life has offered up to this point. I want to commend you for studying hard and for pushing yourself. Your efforts do not deserve to go unnoticed. But the thing is ...

pauses, opens mouth, shuts mouth

exhales and continues

The thing is this: even if you are a university graduate, you don't get to have a cool job (or any job) just because of everything you've done right from primary school until now. You've been given some really bad information about how and why people get hired. Doing everything right is not enough, and your degree doesn't matter nearly as much as you've been told that it does.

What I'm about to say next is messy and complicated and would probably make a brilliant premise for a PhD thesis about reforming the global education system in this 21st century, post-internet, post-recession, knowledge-based economy. But I don't have any interest in doing that PhD — and you don't have that kind of time to burn — so I'm going to do the best I can. (Future PhD candidates of the world, please remember to cite me!)

The modern education system and the modern employment market are not mapped to each other. Not even a little bit, not even vaguely, not even at all. In a perfect supply-and-demand economics vacuum, an entry-level job in fields X or Y would become available in the market each time one person graduated with a degree in X or a qualification in Y. The education system would work much like a factory conveyor belt, one that produced the exact right number of qualified people in all necessary fields. Young people would be trained up to exactly the right level of knowledge needed to integrate seamlessly into their specific and productive role within society. A graduation would trigger the creation of a new job. Or, perhaps, a new job would trigger a graduation.

Did you ever read *The Giver* in school? Where they line up all the kids and tell them which jobs they're going to have for the rest of their lives? For better or worse, we don't live inside that particular dystopia. Instead, in the modern western world, you are encouraged to pursue a formal education where you ultimately study a topic of your choosing. This is a good thing. I think. The employment world, however, continues to hum along regardless of whether you decide to study medicine or French. The world is not magically going to have the right jobs available for the right number of French graduates. There's no butterfly effect rippling through the global economy based on the classes you decide to take. The agency that you have in choosing what to study creates a hiccup (not your fault — the education system's fault!) somewhere along the way:

1. We have a more educated population — score!
2. You can basically choose to study anything you want (grades and finances allowing) — score!
3. We see a lot of educational institutions — universities in particular — claiming that their degrees and qualifications are uniquely valuable, which leads students to assume (incorrectly) that the degree in and of itself will be exchangeable for a job.
4. You graduate, assuming that a job must surely exist somewhere to meet you at this level of achieved effort.

For your whole life as you went through school, this is how the world worked. As soon as you achieved X, you were slotted into the next X+1 level. You finished Year 3 and went into Year 4. You completed secondary school and, based on a set of criteria, there was a university waiting to accept you. And if you did particularly well at any point, a better thing (a higher set or a more prestigious university degree) would be waiting to reward your efforts.

This all stops as soon as academic work stops — but nobody ever really tells you that. You're just supposed to learn a new set of unspoken rules on the fly, often while the grown-ups roll their eyes at you. Transitioning from education to work requires a giant mental reframing. If you've done it recently, you know this. There's the big stuff, like adjusting to working hours, but there are also a lot of subtle glitches in the system that you might not have noticed.

For example, I find it truly frustrating that universities and companies both use the word 'application' when referring to an availability. A university has a guaranteed number of slots available for learners who meet certain criteria, year in and year out. X number of people apply and X-n number of people get in. A company, on the other hand, does not work like this at all. In the world of work, nothing 'happens' just because you decided to switch from medicine to French. There is no next X+1 level waiting for you.

Instead, the employment market is chaos in motion. Entrepreneurs will continue racing around like headless chickens, haphazardly creating new companies which might create some new jobs. There are global organisations that will keep trying to shift and change with the times. There are non-profits that will keep trying to raise money for whatever cause they believe in. There are government agencies that will expand or contract based on the needs of a population and the politics of the day. It's all just particle theory come to life. I was always pretty lousy at science, so to refresh our memories: particle theory, or the kinetic theory of matter, states that all matter consists of many, many, many small particles operating in a continual state of motion. How much any particle moves is determined by the amount of energy it has and its relationship to other particles. Sounds a lot like networking.

Perhaps I've freaked you out. For now, the most important thing to know is that companies are not looking for learners and they are not incentivised to reward you for your past learning. Your new mission is to become excellent at knowing how to make somebody some money or save somebody some time.

Incorrect belief #7: *'I am a university graduate, meaning that I was being groomed for the strategy track. I'll do a little administrative work, but I want to focus on the big-picture stuff.'*

Okay, time to address the big E word: Entitlement.

I genuinely believe that you are hard-working and eager, but I want to stress that you need to be careful when you go around saying stuff like this because it makes you sound entitled, even if you're not.

Career progress will happen quickly and naturally (at any point in your career!) if you possess *all three* of these attributes:

1. Great ideas on how to help the business in a measurable way.
2. The execution skills to bring those ideas to life and produce results.
3. Extraordinary — I'm talking top 1% here — communication skills that allow you to win other people over at every level in the organisation, so that you can scale your influence beyond what you yourself can achieve.

You don't have any of those yet. You couldn't possibly. It's not because you're young, and it's not because you're not capable. It's simply because you don't have any context yet. You don't know how the business (whichever one you'll be working for) actually works. You have no idea what problems you're trying to solve.

For as long as I've been coaching new grads, I've done my best to defend you to all the other grown-ups on this topic. One of my first bosses explained the goal of entry-level work really well to me. It's a rule of thumb that can be applied to the first three to six months of any new job, no matter the seniority level. I'm paraphrasing, but the way he explained it was this: 'You are going to want to score goals, but that is not your job. Your job is to do whatever is needed to help the team score more goals. Your job is to provide defence and maybe make a few good passes. Observe the top strikers who are already on the team, but in the meantime just keep defending.'

I know, I know, you excelled at strategy problems in your exams. But ... the business world is not the same. The business world is the Wild West. You have just joined the circus. Honestly, you're probably on the right track so far, but the physics that guides academics is simply not the same as the physics that guides business. You need to understand that in order to succeed.

Incorrect belief #8: *'I will never be able to get a job in X, because I never formally studied that area.'*
As you already know, this is the extent of my formal academic history:

• Master of Arts in Jazz Vocal Performance
• Bachelor of Arts in English Literature

During my undergraduate degree, the careers advisor asked if I was interested in teaching. I said no. They asked if I wanted to pursue law school. I said no. Their final suggestion was to sign up for missionary work in Africa. And I'm, like, not particularly Christian. When I finished a Master's degree in music, nobody suggested anything at all.

Four years after finishing that Master's degree, I became a beneficiary of the Tier 1 Exceptional Talent Visa (Technology) in the United Kingdom, a prestigious immigration route awarded annually to just 200 technologists — technologist! Me, a jazz singer! — who demonstrate potential to become world leaders in their field. When I was working at Facebook, my last big project involved advising a team of back-end engineers through the process of reorganising a crucial part of the codebase. If that sounds like crazy technical gibberish that has nothing to do with your field of interest, please don't worry.

My point is this: a little bit at a time, I taught myself all the skills I needed along the way. I was not doomed just because I studied music. On the flipside, my degrees are not the sole reasons I succeeded either. Both of my degrees are, at the end of the day, just something I chose to do with one chapter of my life. And, because of how time works, they slowly fade into the distance as I continue to write more chapters of my story.

Over the years, through every good job and not-so-good job, I always wanted to understand more about how all the dots connected. I fell into 'technology' stuff completely by accident, because I kept wondering what the team in the next room over was doing all day long. My curiosity has always been my biggest professional advantage. I have naturally spotted opportunities to grow my skillset, even in toxic and restrictive environments, because I am always genuinely interested in the big picture.

The curious will win over the educated, every time.

Incorrect belief #9: *'The next degree will make me stand out. I should go get my MBA (or whatever).'*
You're probably spotting a pattern to what I think about degrees by now, but let's really hammer in the point with this one: *a degree does not guarantee you a job offer.*

Here are the good reasons to go get an MBA (or whatever):
- You have identified a specific job that strictly requires this specific degree.
- You understand that you learn better in traditionally structured environments and you are prepared to pay for that structure in both time and money.

- You want to get on the executive management track in a large corporation (the MBA is not always a requirement, but it's still pretty common).
- You want to tap into this specific university's alumni network and are excited to be a part of this specific university's community.

Here are the wrong reasons to go get an MBA (or whatever):
- You hate your job and you just want to take a break.
- You feel lost and you don't know what to do next.
- You are failing at getting hired and think that this degree will do the trick.
- You feel trapped in your job and you want to hit the do-over button.
- Your parents think it's the safe thing to do.
- Your parents are worried that you haven't got married yet and they think it will be easier for you to find a partner in an academic setting (I've heard this more than once).

Getting another degree won't automatically get you hired. Learning how to get hired — and understanding why people get hired — will get you hired.

Doctors and other professions that require a specific qualification, obviously ignore me on this one. Everybody else, please heed my advice. Be critical about whether or not that degree is actually necessary, or if you're just hoping it will help. The worst-case situation here is that you will have wasted a couple years of earning potential, you will be deep in debt, and you will still not be able to get hired.

There is a quiet, growing trend of global companies getting rid of their requirement *even for an undergraduate degree*. While you might expect that from Silicon Valley companies like Google and Apple — both of which have gone on the record to say degrees are not a requirement for most of their top positions — the trend has already spread far and wide. As Maggie Stilwell, then Ernst & Young's managing partner for talent, explained in a 2015 interview for HuffPost: 'Academic qualifications will still be taken into account and indeed remain an important consideration when assessing candidates as a whole, but will no longer act as a barrier to getting a foot in the door.'

To be clear, the trend towards ditching degrees does not mean you don't need skills. You definitely need skills — lots of them — and you'll probably need to learn new ones from time to time. But you rarely need a traditional degree in order to obtain said skills. Got me?

Incorrect belief #10: *'I can only apply for internships, because I don't have any official experience yet and internships are the only way to get official experience that counts.'*
Nope. The concept of 'official experience' is a false idol, and it's not dissimilar to the idea that you have to do the 'right' kind of degree in order to work in certain fields.

An internship is a great way to get experience, but it's not your only option. We'll go through several techniques in Step 2 for adding skills into your toolkit on the fly. For now, just know that there are so many ways to demonstrate proficiency. Whether you take up volunteering, tackle a strategically helpful extracurricular initiative at your current job, or spend every night watching YouTube tutorials until you really grasp the subject matter, your learning is going to be in your hands from here on out.

Nobody can ever stop you from learning. Not in this day and age, not on my watch.

Incorrect belief #11: *'I don't have any skills. I am an unemployable disaster.'*

Everybody has some kind of super talent that can be harnessed to get them ahead. If you're lucky, these talents are obvious. A triple axel in freestyle figure-skating, for example, or the ability to fit more marshmallows in your mouth than any of your friends can. Other talents — most, in fact — require a bit of an archaeological dig.

Over the course of any job search, it's tempting to fool yourself into thinking that you need to acquire a brand-new set of skills (or a new personality) in a desperate attempt to tick off every candidate requirement you come across. In reality, the first skill you need to acquire is the ability to explain why the skills you have right now, today, are valuable. If you can't do this, you will never be able to explain why any new skills you acquire are valuable either. This is the argument I use with anyone who tells me they need another degree in order to get hired, by the way. If you couldn't explain why you'll be helpful the first time around, why would anything change with a second piece of paper?

If you can identify your own skills and explain yourself to others, you can do anything. Pair this narrative-spinning magic with a willingness to teach yourself new skills over the course of your career, and you become unstoppable.

Incorrect belief #12: *'I should only apply for jobs at companies whose names I recognise because those are the most prestigious jobs.'*

Many of us are instinctively drawn to working for companies we've heard of before.

'I work for Coca-Cola!' you can imagine yourself saying. 'You know … the world-famous beverage company!' The security of brand recognition feels good. You could tell anyone in the world that you work for this company, and they'll know just what you mean.

Look, just because you've *had* a Coke, doesn't mean you know a single thing about what it's like to work for the company behind the beverage. And just because you haven't heard of Some Smaller Company You've Never Heard Of doesn't mean a thing. The stranger across the street might very well be your soulmate, feel me?

Be wary of logo blindness. You will miss a good thing that's right in front of you.

Incorrect belief #13: *'No companies are hiring right now. It's the wrong time of year.'*
Companies are not like universities, companies are not like universities, companies are not like universities.

There is no single application cycle that every employer out there has agreed to stick to so that all the new grads know where to go on their first day of the autumn term. Every company's hiring patterns and timelines are entirely unique. The world is chaos come to life, there's a lot going on. If you Google 'best time to look for a job', you will overwhelmingly get the impression that most hiring happens from January to April. That's a much too simplified answer, but it's based on something more important that will be really helpful for you to understand during the search process: headcount planning.

Alexa, what's headcount planning?
So glad you asked.

In the autumn, many companies start making decisions about how many open roles they need to fill in the next year. This process, sometimes referred to as headcount planning, is based on a lot of different factors: revenue growth projections, new projects the company wants to invest in, people getting promoted, people leaving the company, etc.

Based on this, a company comes up with a number. They may release these roles over time (it would be hard for some companies to train 20 new people simultaneously), but most companies attempt to have a set prediction in place for the entire year. Because of money. The company needs to know how much money it is going to spend on its people.

Once the budget gets decided (example: we're going to hire five people at £30k per person for an estimated salary budget increase of £150k), it gets difficult for a hiring manager to just 'find' other money that hasn't been spoken for elsewhere in the company. While it can be tempting to think that every rejection or 'we're not hiring right now' response is a personal affront to you and your character, it's usually got a lot more to do with these predetermined annual budget allocations. Employees make the world go round — and they're also just an expense that needs to be accounted for in a company's financial reports. Understanding how hiring works is an invaluable asset during the job search.

(I'm very proud to report that I had an accounting friend read over this particular myth. Her response: 'As someone who has managed headcount forecasting in a major Fortune 500 company, this is exactly true.')

Incorrect belief #14: *'Tomorrow, I will figure everything out and my new life will start.'*
I like to refer to this particular belief as the Movie Montage Phenomenon.

> **Movie Montage Phenomenon** = the unrealistic thought that, once you decide on the 'right' path, you will immediately enter into a period of frenzied achievement during which you work hard in a total vacuum and then, 90 seconds and one uplifting song later, achieve your goals and complete nirvana all in one go. (See: that scene in *Legally Blonde* where she goes dressed as a bunny to buy the MacBook and then studies really hard on the elliptical trainer.)

You will not magically figure out life in one day and then go out into the real world to execute your entire vision in one fell swoop. You will figure out your life by trial and error, just like the rest of us.

Careers require action. Taking action is scary if you don't know where to start. Luckily for both of us, you have this book. You have me. I'm going to help. Let's go and get started.

Employers, they're just like us

Employers and job seekers are star-crossed lovers. They are but two lost souls reaching out, desperately yearning, trying to grasp for each other's hands in the dark.

As it goes with Tinder, as it goes with LinkedIn: there is a human being sitting on the other side of the computer screen, and they likely aren't very good at this either. It takes two to tango, and all of us seem to have two left feet. Why must we suck at communicating with the very people we need most? Seeking work and seeking love both seem to have this uncanny knack for transforming us into fumbling lunatics. I know that I, for one, feel just as doomed to drown in missed connections, subtext, and ghosted goodbyes during the hiring process as I do on a third date. It's tragic.

To illustrate just how bad we are at this, I invite you to take a moment and reflect back on a recent romantic crush. I'll go first:

I … am in love. I wasn't sure about him for the first ten minutes after we met at that party, but then I noticed how sexy his smile was, and when we started joking about music — I mean, what are the odds that we both like music *and* podcasts? Insane. Sometimes you almost write off the love of your life, it's so crazy!

We have texted 12 times in the last seven weeks. Not that I counted. We were supposed to go to dinner, but then he cancelled, and so then we went to lunch, but that's honestly so much more *intimate. I felt real butterflies. I wonder when his birthday is. He's so funny. Plus, he mentioned his sister to me, so I'm assuming that he wants us to meet? I hope I get along with her, it's so hard when you have to force a relationship with the family. Anyway, I *think* we're on the same page. There was a lot left unsaid in our eye contact. Eeeek, sometimes you just know, you know? It honestly feels written in the stars. I don't think it's outer-limits to say we might actually be engaged to wed by the time this book goes to print. PLEASE SEND BLESSINGS FOR MY UPCOMING NUPTIALS, I'M PLANNING A NEW YEAR'S EVE WEDDING!*

When those pheromones kick in, you are blinded. The wanting shrouds logical thought. *This* is how you get your happily-ever-after, you think. You quickly construct an entire life in your mind. You become so focused on getting the other party's attention that you forget to remember that the object of your affection is a perfectly imperfect person, the same as you. Instead, this person becomes a voodoo doll of sorts. They look human on the surface, but they're actually a complex emotional fabrication woven from the threads of your dreams and cushioned on a pillowy bed of fantasies.

You read into every text. You draw connections where there are none. You weigh the pros and cons of a grand romantic gesture. You pace around your bedroom, waiting for them to come to their senses, pick up the phone, and call to say, 'It's you! It's always been you! I can't do this without you, I never should have doubted it, I want you to know that I'm ready and you're …

'… hired.'

Because it *is* the same, isn't it? When dating employers (that's what a job search really is), we are so quick to put the dream job up on a pedestal — right there on the shelf next to that one person in Maths class who never loved us back.

We want to believe in the perfection of the employer. With their sexy logos and cool-kid mission statements, it's easy to develop these professional crushes. All the well-coiffed employees in those photos appear to be the chosen ones. *Look at them, smiling. They probably made more strategic decisions about their extracurriculars at the age of 13. I should have played the violin.*

Herein lies the chaotic but liberating truth: all employers are imperfect because all companies (or organisations or non-profits or government branches or whatever) are imperfect.

Coca-Cola began as a hare-brained scheme to market and sell a mixture of drugs, sugar, and caffeine. Google supposedly started in that garage. Alexander McQueen ran his entire company as a side hustle for five years (including the year he sold a majority stake to Gucci Group, how?). Tesco started out as a grocer's stall in Hackney. Marriott opened with just two East Coast motels. Every company, if you trace it back to its origins, is basically somebody's good idea that got a little out of hand.

In order to make the next sale, companies are constantly making it up on the fly. They find new people to help. The new people help them find new customers. Decades pass. They get listed on the stock exchange or something. They have a Careers page of their own, and a whole team of people exclusively dedicated to finding even more new people to help them make the next sale. All companies are made up, they're imperfect. These imperfect entities shall be the metaphorical lily pads between which you leapfrog during the course of your career.

A lot of famous military leaders have written about the need to intimately understand one's opponent. In *The Art of War*, Sun Tzu wrote: 'Victorious warriors win first and then go to war, while defeated warriors go to war first and then seek to win.' I am not a famous military leader (yet), but this is what I want you to do: you, my friend, *need* to understand how hiring looks from the other party's perspective.

A relationship is rarely broken for just one person. For the next few pages, I am going to lay bare several problems that employers are grappling with over on their side of the table. I want you to step out of the Matrix and see the world from a new perspective. I want you to picture yourself as the person across the table — the one who wrote the job description, the one who's reading your application, the one who uploaded your CV into a folder for somebody else to read, the one who's scheduling the interviews.

The one who's out there, right now, tasked with trying to find *you*.

Understanding the enemy

We just debunked 14 myths about how employment works from the job seeker's perspective, so you can imagine that there's an equally long list of misconceptions on the employer's side, too.

To demonstrate, let's consider the two most common assets required for a job application: a cover letter and a CV. Everybody asks for the same thing, whether the vacancy is for an actuary, a paralegal, a supermarket manager, or a hair stylist. If you went out and asked these employers why — in this, the modern age of possibility and Wi-Fi — they are requesting these specific documents, you would see a pattern emerge very quickly.

It's the way they've always done things.

For any company that existed before the internet, hiring was probably the least of their worries once the digital revolution was underway. While putting out a thousand other fires, they hastily digitised their process by asking you to email them instead of sending in a real letter.

For any company that was founded after the internet, hiring was probably the least of their worries while they figured out how to sell whatever it was they were selling. They didn't have time to reinvent the wheel. They just mimicked what everybody else was doing. And besides, every company that had come before them seemed to be upholding the status quo. If it ain't broke, don't fix it, right?

I ask every recruiter and hiring manager I meet to tell me what they hate most about the hiring process. The gist of it is that they feel like they're drowning. They wish they could keep better track of the CVs they get sent. They wish they had a better system of going back to find the people they rejected six months ago, to see if those candidates would be interested in going through the interview process again. They wish they had a better way to find people who are looking for new opportunities.

But who's got time to fix the system? Who even knows where to start? Everybody's got a new role to fill, and a process that sort of works, and that's going to have to be good enough for today. Recruiters (or whoever's in charge of hiring — it varies wildly from company to company!) are often 'graded' at their job based on quantitative metrics, like how many candidates they can find and put forward for interview. Stopping the recruitment process to re-evaluate how it's done would potentially decrease this number for a certain period of time. That's not an easy risk to take, even for the most innovative companies in the world — but there is a price to pay for maintaining the status quo.

Raise your hand if you've recently given in to the temptation to fire off your CV simply because the application didn't require a cover letter. Spamming out job descriptions online — on job boards, LinkedIn, etc. — is the employer version of this temptation. They don't even need to copy and paste a new company name on the top to do it. I often overhear recruiters talking about finding candidates the same way they'd talk about doing digital marketing for a shiny new product. 'Let's get some exposure for this vacancy,' they might say. 'We need to get this out there immediately. Where can we post it online?'

The largest employers all have their own slick Careers sites that they update with new jobs postings. What you might not know, however, is that building and maintaining that kind of website costs a lot more money and time than you'd think. It's a luxury that many small to medium-sized employers can't afford, which is why websites like LinkedIn have become so popular. Aggregate job sites help companies to hire by providing a low-cost solution that makes publishing a job posting online as easy as clicking a button. Signing up for these services is cheap and fast. The employer pays a nominal fee to publish their job postings for a certain amount of time or a certain number of views. (It's not dissimilar to, say, posting a classified ad in the local paper.)

As you might imagine, it's incredibly tempting to post the same job listing on multiple sites so that you get a lot of eyeballs on it very quickly. And even if you fill that vacancy within two weeks, you might have paid for the posting to show up online for 30 days. The employers who are really on top of things may remember to take down the listing once they find their candidate, but that's not going to be the top priority on their to-do list. In some cases, the money for the ad has already been spent, so they might as well move on to this week's projects.

If you've put two and two together, you've already spotted the problem. You, job seeker, could easily be spending a lot of time and emotional labour and anxiety energy applying for a position that was already filled last month. Whoops.

The karmic retribution employers must face, though, is figuring out how to deal with your *incoming* spam. Can you imagine trying to figure out which are the good candidates when you receive 70 applications in a week? What about if you receive 700 or 7,000? What about when most of those candidates seem to have no clue what your company does and didn't even manage to update the name of the position in their cover letter? A needle in a haystack doesn't even begin to cover it.

Recruiters have no magical way to deal with what surely must feel like a tidal wave of applications, day in and day out, and they definitely don't have time to read between the lines of your application and try to piece together whether or not you've got what it takes to do the job. You, a total stranger. Just one application out of 700, sitting in their inbox among all the rest. They're bound to get fatigued.

This application overload is why a lot of recruiters have created their own list of very dumb deal-breakers. Submit your application in a hard-to-read font? Next. Use the word *guru* or *influencer* in your cover letter? Next. You can't fault them for moving so quickly. They need to get through this inbox and find something vaguely resembling a promising candidate, before the next tidal wave hits tomorrow.

Meanwhile, on the other side of the screen, you're starting to get getting antsy. *I sent in my CV two days ago. Should I follow up today?*

When you're looking for a job and every single day feels crucial, it's so tempting to beat yourself up about not getting hired fast enough. The assumption is that something must be wrong with your application — unless, wait, are these recruiters just screwing with you on purpose? Don't they know that you've put yourself on house arrest while you wait for a reply? Don't they realise that you are nobly chained to your laptop, prepared to immediately head to the office as soon as they finally call (and surely they'll call tomorrow)?

The timeline looks a lot different from the hiring side. Headcount planning (see page 18) is based on annual budgets. Recruiters set monthly or quarterly goals for getting new people in through the door. There's also just the general chaos of life, of course. The people that are tasked with hiring you are also trying to manage their own personal and professional schedules. Your recruiter may have sworn that the team was going to make a decision by this Thursday, but then he forgot to send out an update before he boarded the plane to his cousin's wedding in France and now his out-of-office message says he'll be gone for ten days. While that kind of behaviour won't win him any awards, it's a pretty common situation.

I gave a talk once to a room full of people who wanted to discuss how to expand the digital economy in the United Kingdom. 'Raise your hand if you got paid to be here today,' I started. Everyone in the room awkwardly put their hands up. 'Now, raise your hand if you have a stack of unanswered emails from candidates who want to work for you sitting in your inbox. How long have you been ignoring them? And how many times have you groaned about how hard it is to hire this week? They want to help you grow your company — and you're sitting here, talking to me, as if all those people have time to kill.'

Bad job descriptions provide yet another major opportunity for missed connections. I think I was 25 the first time I got hired to write a job description. The request came from the VP of talent at a company I had done some marketing work for in the past. 'Would you consider helping us improve our job description template?' she asked me. 'We have some really crucial open roles and we want to look more polished!'

Until this point, even though I was a freelance copywriter, it honestly hadn't occurred to me that job descriptions were just haphazard pieces of text crafted by real human hands. I viewed each and every job posting as a holy decree of all the skills I still needed to master before I was allowed to even consider sending in an application. Oh, how wrong I was.

There are a variety of reasons why you shouldn't take a job description at face value. For one, recruiters aren't always the most talented writers. Or whoever wrote the job description might have been unfamiliar with the skillset required for that role. They might have just collaged some words together based on what their competitor's job postings look like. Trust me, I've sat in rooms and watched these kinds of things happen.

The most important thing to know is that any candidate requirements you come across are not really requirements at all. Those bullet points are simply a dreamt-up idea of what the perfect candidate might look like. See also: 'Ummm, I guess, like, 6 foot 1 and broad-shouldered; blue or green eyes; he should have a quirky sense of humour and a great relationship with his mum; oh, he should love surprising me with little gifts …'

At its core, a job description is a CV, but in reverse. It is a marketing tool designed to pique interest from the right people. All any company is ever trying to say with a job description is: 'We need someone who kind of knows about this kind of stuff, who could help us do something kind of like this. We think that's what we need, anyway. Is it you?'

Accepting an imperfect process

Time and again throughout this book, I will encourage you to think about the human being sitting on the other side of the computer reading your application. I will ask you to put yourself in their shoes, platonically flirt with them, show empathy for them, and brighten their day.

They still might not pick you. And one of the very hardest things to accept about this process is that, many times, employers simply get it wrong.

Your dream employer will pick the wrong candidate when they should have picked you. You will want to bang your head against the wall. You will have flashbacks to James, the crush you shared insane chemistry with, the one with whom things just clicked, I mean, you were compatible and you shared all the same values ... and he didn't see how obviously perfect you were for each other. It was right there in front of him. JAMES, C'MON MAN, IT WAS RIGHT THERE.

Employers will make the wrong choice for a thousand different reasons. There will be the obvious and really stupid reasons. There will be unconscious bias and deeply unfair discrimination. But sometimes, you just won't get the job and there will be no good (or bad) reason why. Let me illustrate:

When I was living in San Francisco and stalking the internet in preparation for my big move to Berlin, I thought I had discovered the perfect company. The sensation was akin to realising that soulmates existed. My background mapped perfectly to what they needed *and* they were in the same industry as my current employer *and* they were hiring. Cosmic was, in my opinion, an understatement. I even excitedly told some San Francisco about-to-be-ex-co-workers about the company I had discovered. *I think this is going to be a competitor of ours someday!* Nobody had heard of them.

I cold-emailed one of their employees to introduce myself. I scored a networking meeting for my first week in Berlin. We talked shop. We brainstormed some awesome ideas. We vibed. We drank beer together! Over the next month, I pitched the team a couple of ideas for how I could help. I heard nothing. I submitted a formal application. I heard nothing. I followed up. I followed up again. I got ghosted. I'm pretty sure they hired their summer intern, a woman who (I think) had become popular in the office and probably did an okay enough job in the role. I will go on record, even today, in print, in this book which will sit on someone's bookshelf somewhere for decades to come, to say that I would have been a stronger hire. I know it down to my bones.

Not three years later, that San Francisco ex-employer and this Berlin company went on to announce a huge collaborative partnership. Please remember that neither of them had heard of each other in 2014.

bangs head against the wall, very loudly

In spite of all of that, I will argue that this company made the right hiring choice — because the right hiring choice and choosing the best candidate are not actually synonymous.

I was taught, growing up, that the best person should always get the job, and if that didn't happen, it was because of something super bad like racism or nepotism. So long as things are going well and nobody tries to get away with anything evil, the best person for the job will be hired. Imagine my surprise when I found out that — and this is mathematically proven — the best candidate gets the job just over one third of the time.

A famous probability principle, often referred to as the 37% Rule or the Secretary Problem, can help us understand (and, ultimately, accept) this particular brand of chaos.

Imagine that you're hiring a new secretary. You want to hire the best possible applicant. You get to interview the applicants in a random order, but you must make a decision immediately following each and every interview. Assume that if you offer any applicant the job, they are guaranteed to accept. If you pass, the applicant disappears forever. How do you make your decision? The situation is precarious. You become less and less interested in figuring out which candidate is truly the best, and more interested in simply figuring out how you'll know that you have found someone *good enough*. Do you keep looking for love and risk waiting to find out that soulmates don't exist, or do you start a family with this perfectly nice person right now? It's your call.

The optimal strategy for choosing a secretary turns out to be what Brian Christian and Tom Griffiths refer to as the Look-Then-Leap Rule in *Algorithms To Live By* — and the methodology is exactly as imperfect as it sounds. You decide on a set period of time during which you exclusively try to understand what your options are and don't choose anyone, even if they appear to be excellent. As soon as the clock strikes twelve, you 'enter the "leap" phase, prepared to instantly commit' to the next good option you come across. This is where the 37% Rule comes into play.

By running the maths, Christian and Griffiths conclude that 'the exact place to draw the link between looking and leaping settles to 37% of the pool, yielding the 37% Rule: look at the first 37% of the applicants, choosing none, then be ready to leap for anyone better than all those you've seen so far'. The maths remains the same no matter how big the pool gets. Sobering odds.

While your first reaction might be hopelessness, I see a silver lining in the madness. Companies are forever balancing finding the best candidate for the job and going with the best candidate they've found so far — which means they are statistically likely to pick somebody too early rather than wait for the right person. After all, 'the whole time you're searching for a secretary, you don't have a secretary. What's more, you're spending the day conducting interviews instead of getting your own work done.'

Is it all chaos? In a word, yes.

As a consultant or freelancer, I've worked with dozens of companies over the course of my career. I've never not heard someone say, 'Welcome! Things are crazy around here, haha!' on my first day in a new office. Understanding the humanity and the madness of the hiring process, however, helps us to see our future employers and colleagues as fellow humans rather than faceless decision-makers. Plus, if you can identify glitches in the Matrix as they happen, you can begin to see hidden opportunities for bending the spoon.

At the end of the day, every office is filled to the brim with plain-old humans — some of whom dislike their job as much as you might dislike yours. Doesn't matter whether it's FedEx or the CIA, some guy named Tom is sitting around killing time on Reddit and figuring out how to leave early on Friday. Or trying to get to work on time during rush hour. Or planning out their annual leave. Or scrambling at the last minute to finish a project they procrastinated on until last night. Or picking the wrong person for the role.

You will continue to get infatuated with the wrong companies and get fixated on the wrong roles and get excited about first interviews that never turn into anything more. You are human, and this is what it is to look for work. That's okay. But it's time to take your future employer — and, more importantly, the rigor of this process — down off that pedestal.

Whenever you feel hurt, like you're not enough, like you've done something wrong, or like you should be embarrassed for having applied at all, I want you to remember all the things I've said to you today. The job search may feel like having a whole bunch of crushes reject you in a row, but know that there's an imperfect human waiting to meet you, too.

And, remember, she's just an employer. Sitting in front of her laptop. Asking you to love her.

Part 2

Preparing For Battle

*A woodsman was once asked, 'What would you do if you
had just five minutes to chop down a tree?'
He answered, 'I would spend the first two and a half
minutes sharpening my axe.'*

I had no idea who Wilt Chamberlain was until I heard his story on This American Life, the NPR podcast, and realised that he has a whole lot in common with you, the job seeker reading this book.

Wilt Chamberlain is widely considered to be one of the best basketball players of all time, apart from his terrible free-throw percentage. In basketball, free throws are an opportunity to score points by shooting unopposed from behind the foul line, usually as a result of your team being awarded a penalty. The free-throw thing is particularly important because that's what turned Wilt Chamberlain into the star of a parable that's now told all over the world.

Here's what happened:

Chamberlain sucked at free throws. But, with help from fellow ballplayer Rick Barry, he famously changed technique before starting the 1961–62 season and brought his free-throw percentage up to a career-best 61% average. He scored more free throws in a single game (28 out of 32) than anyone ever had in the history of the sport. By the following season, however, he had given the technique up entirely.

Rick Barry had taught Chamberlin how to shoot underhanded, a method often referred to as *granny style*. Shooting that way, Chamberlain said, was embarrassing. It made him feel like a sissy. And so he went back to doing things the old way and, predictably, his free-throw percentage declined back to where it had been before. He never again shot as well as he did during the 1961–62 season when he'd been brave enough to try something else.

The desire to follow the crowd is so strong that we will hold ourselves back on purpose just to blend in with what everybody else seems to be doing. We revert to the ineffective choice even when we've discovered a better way to go about things.

I think about that a lot.

The mainstream approach to finding a job has not worked for you up until this point. As we just spoke about in Part 1, that's not entirely your fault. In this book, I'm going to be the Rick Barry to your Wilt Chamberlain. I'm going teach you a better technique for career success and, unlike Chamberlain, you're going to be brave enough to use it.

Starting today, your job search strategy looks like this:

1. You'll become crystal clear on what you're trying to accomplish. You'll be able to name the exact companies and organisations you want to work for, and the exact job you want to do for said companies and organisations.
2. You'll do the prep work required to become extremely hireable by those companies and organisations.
3. You'll proactively and methodically introduce yourself to the right people until you get hired.

This strategy might sound so intimidating that you are already convinced you're now just going to fail at the job search from another angle. Alternatively, it might sound so obvious and achievable that you no longer feel the need to read the rest of this book. Either way, you need to give yourself permission to shoot underhanded and see what happens. This is all I ask of you.

But before we begin for real, I have a few ground rules I'd like to lay down, because — after all — you're playing ball on my court from here on out.

The ground rules

1. Quit the job-search junk-food diet today.

No more applications, at least until you read through Part 2 and figure out how to sharpen your axe. None. Until you know exactly what you want and you are prepared to put your best foot forward, we do not need you out there frantically hurling CVs at people.

You are only allowed to continue conversations that are already underway. You are not allowed to start any new conversations, send out any new CVs, or submit any new applications until you complete all of the task list items assigned to you at the ends of Steps 1–5.

2. Schedule in your job search tasks — and schedule in your off-time, too.

'I can't come,' I said matter-of-factly. 'I'm job searching.'

It was my best friend from university, calling from New York. No one had heard from me in weeks, and she wanted to make sure I had booked my flights for the weekend away everyone had agreed on. 'Lex, the weekend we're talking about is three months away. Please. It's the first time we'll all be together again since graduation. This is important.'

I couldn't hear her through that panicky fog that often accompanies unemployment (or underemployment or hate-your-employment). All of my instincts said I needed to stay right where

I was, in case the Big Call came in from Some Boss who was about to offer me Some Job at Some Company. I couldn't be busy — ever. I needed to wait by the phone. I needed to be ready to report for duty.

If that sounds familiar to you, I want you to hear me loud and clear: if anyone ever calls you on a Friday afternoon and tells you that you need to start working at 4pm that very same day or else they're rescinding the offer — well, first of all, I will pay you £5 if that actually happens. For real, though, if this fictitious company refuses to hire you unless you come back early from a weekend trip with your friends, something is off. You are dealing with a massive red flag situation and you do not want that job.

I demand that you keep living your life while you look for work. You will not make this process go faster by chaining yourself to the desk.

I want you to set a weekly (or daily) goal that's *significantly* more tangible than Find A New Job. Your unemployment anxiety spirals are unproductive. As you go through the task lists for each Step, you'll develop an ongoing list of tangible goals. Your assignment might be something like 'Call three family friends and set a date for coffee' or 'Refine that skills section on my CV' or 'Spell-check and publish my online portfolio' or 'Complete the full application for X position'.

Once you have completed your goal, step away from the computer. Stop. You're not doing yourself any favours by 'working' (AKA browsing job descriptions) from morning to night. You did enough. You're done. If you're following my plan and you're consistently assigning yourself 45-minute chunks of homework based on the task lists, you're making progress. As Ralph Waldo Emerson once wrote in a letter to his daughter, 'Finish each day and be done with it. You have done what you could.'

You'll be a healthier person, and a less desperate candidate, because of it.

3. Find a hobby and/or learn a new professional skill.

I hereby ban you from spending your extra time browsing through job descriptions. Use all those extra hours to become a more employable person. We'll dig into what I mean in Step 2. What if you're already super-employable and have more skills than a Swiss army knife? First of all, the economy is changing so quickly that this feels extremely unlikely. But if that's really what you're working with, then I want you to get a hobby. I can't begin to tell you how lame you're going to feel if, when the interview finally does come, you don't have an answer for the So What Have You Been Up To Recently question. (*What have I been up to? I've been sitting at home, waiting for you to schedule this interview, that's what!!* is not a good conversation starter.)

4. Stop trying to latch your star onto somebody else's.

A lot of us let our careers just … *happen* to us.

It goes like this: You get offered your first job. Your boss tells you that they always wished they'd done a rotation in X department, and that's what they recommend you do, if you think you'd be interested in it. You always kind of liked it when your teachers would tell you what to do next, so why not listen to this person? You do the rotation. Your next boss tells you she thinks you're just perfect for her role, since she's about to get promoted. You figure it's a move in the right direction. You take the job. Your mum says you should go get an MBA, and then your dad says you should really consider taking that management position. You do those things, too. And so on.

The easiest route through life is to follow good advice. It's not necessarily laziness so much as an optimistic hope that we'll some day come across a Real Grown-Up who actually knows What The Hell Is Going On. And so we catch ourselves saying to the world again and again, 'Here are my skills. What do you think I should do with them?'

The job search exacerbates this habit, so I need you to repeat this mantra to yourself again and again: *I am the only one who can make a decision about what to do next.*

Many times over the course of your life, it's possible that *you* are going to be the only person you've ever known who's encountered this particular career decision. No one else will know what to do. You will have to make a decision by yourself, and no amount of brain-picking or advice-asking is ever going to feel like enough. The next kind soul to buy you a coffee will not be able to tell you what to do with your life. These people will, however, be able to provide answers to specific questions. More on that once we get into networking.

5. Just f*cking ship it.
If you aren't familiar with the phrase, 'ship it' is software development lingo for, basically, pushing the button that publishes the most recent version of your website or app or feature live. The phrase has become an industry joke of sorts. The equivalent of saying, 'Do you feel ready? I don't. Anyway, here goes nothing.'

Every industry has their own version of this advice. Someone told me once that you're never actually finished recording an album — you just run out of time or money. During the process of writing this book, someone else told me a manuscript is only done when the editor gently pries it out of your hands. I've heard entrepreneur friends say that, if you're not a little bit embarrassed on the day that you launch your company, you probably waited too long. Done is better than perfect.

I was once talking a friend through an application she was sending out for a job she really wanted. She's a designer. Her portfolio — which is always the hardest part — was stunning. Her website looked slick. The cover letter was solid. She was ready to rock, and then she told me she wanted to redo her website and look over her portfolio again before she submitted anything. I took a deep breath and said, 'Please just send it in. Now. Or tomorrow. Give yourself a deadline. Because how silly are you going to feel if you wait another three weeks, get everything ready and totally perfect, go to apply and — oh wait, they've already taken the job posting down because someone else got there faster than you?'

Just f*cking ship it. This is the mantra I want you to repeat to yourself if your instinct is to want to wait until tomorrow when you're a little bit more prepared. I understand that you don't want to just half-arse it, fail, and realise you could have done more. That's a commendable behaviour in a lot of ways. And maybe it will work out perfectly to really take your time, put in all the hard work you can possibly think of, and reap the fruits of your labour six to eight months from now. But most of the time? Opportunities have sell-by dates, even for the most talented among us. When you say you 'need more time', your potential future employer is most likely hearing, 'I'm not ready. Ask somebody else.'

You're never all-the-way ready. You have to take action any-way. In order to get hired, you need to *send* the email. You need to *make* the appointment. You need to *hit submit* on that application. Set your goals, hit your deadlines, and let's go do the thing. You deserve to take your shot just as much as anybody else does. Go and f*cking ship it.

6. Stop listening to advice from people whose careers you do not want.

A few years back, I read something on Instagram that hit me like a ton of bricks: 'Average talent works really hard to fit in. Exceptional talent works really, really hard to stand out.' The second half of this sentence isn't what hit me. It's the first part — about talented people who are out there trying their absolute best with the primary goal of blending into the crowd.

Many of us grew up learning that hating your job, stressing about your job, and thinking your job is boring are all normal feelings. And because 'everybody' thinks like that, we all go along with it. When I was going through my Worst Year Ever in San Francisco, I got a lot of well-intentioned bad advice that stemmed from this train of thought. Friends and family told me to live for the weekend, pointed out to me that jobs aren't always that fun, tried to recommend TV shows for me to get hooked on. I got told, frequently, to just shut down my brain in order to get through the day. I kept thinking, *I'm so unhappy I can't see straight. Surely this is not how this is all supposed to go down from now until forever. I'm not buying it.*

As it turns out, I was right. I was not crazy for being unhappy or unfulfilled, and neither are you. Deciding in my gut that I didn't buy into the 'hating your job is normal' game was the first step towards building a better, stronger, dare I say delightful career path for myself.

I really want the same for you. I have built a life in which I roll deep in a passionate community of friends and peers who utterly adore their work. A lot of media articles would have you believe that these people are all entrepreneurs and artists, but they're not. The majority of them have full-time jobs, and I watch them get dorky-excited about all the projects they're working on. I want you to start picturing the possibility that you could be one of these people too. They exist.

In order to give this job search thing your best shot, you need to pay close attention to how the people around you talk about their jobs. Gravitate towards those who get excited — and, with grace, commit to giving yourself some space from the people who don't get it. You are allowed to stray from the crowd, at least for a little while, until you get hired.

7. Stop thinking 'I'm not working' is the same thing as 'Nobody wants me'.

If you're unemployed or deeply underemployed, I want you to hear me loud and clear: you are going to get a job. It is extremely unlikely that you are the one truly unemployable person on this earth. I know you're worried, I know you're panicking about money, I know you're exhausted, I know you feel like a failure. Please believe me when I tell you that your panic will not get you hired any faster.

I know how hard it can be to get going when you don't have a lot on the calendar. Which is why, to really snap you out of it and show you the possibilities, I want to tell you about how Antoine, a startup executive who is now based in London, approached one of his most difficult job searches early on in his career:

> I wasn't working, so I used that time to really level up. I cross-referenced job descriptions from the jobs I wanted, and if they referenced anything I wasn't familiar with, I would spend a day understanding the basics. Even for the ones I did know, I would use the time to practise that skill. I wanted to accumulate knowledge. I found people in my industry to follow online. I found one person who had a list of recommended books and I read every single one.
>
> Even though I really had fun doing it, there came a point when I realised I couldn't spend more than two to three hours a day job hunting, even with learning stuff. I knew that, for the job I wanted, this process could take a few months. I thought, 'Okay, what do I like doing? I like surfing.' So I found an eco-hostel on the coast in Mexico — I was living in Mexico City at the time — and I job searched from the palapa on the beach in the morning and surfed in the afternoons. I think that not obsessing about the outcome really helped me to move faster. I ultimately did the interview

for the job I have now from that hostel. Time went by quickly because I was enjoying myself. It's good to take a step back, do what you love, and enjoy the downtime for what it is.

Whether or not you can make it to the beach, cut yourself some slack and go do something fun. Create a schedule for yourself, stick to the plan, and say this out loud every day if you need to: *I am setting myself up for success. I am putting in the work. This new job thing is going to work itself out very soon.*

Okay, I think we're ready. You know the rules. Let's begin.

Step 1: The Target Employer List

At the time this book went to press, there were *20 million* active job postings on LinkedIn alone. Just on that one site. Never in the history of the world have we had access to this much professional opportunity at our fingertips.

But this access to opportunity — perceived or legitimate — can be distracting. Paralysingly so. I find that the lure of limitless possibilities confuses the mind. Every job posting you see is a glimpse into the new life you could have, or should have, or could have had if you hadn't already made the decisions that brought you to where you are today. It's an existential crisis minefield. And the fact that you're trying to sift through this level of information overload while jacked up on the adrenaline and shame which we know pair so nicely with a job search? Nasty.

When we're wading through this kind of mental mud, we often resort to making rapid movement of any kind instead of pausing to come up with a better strategy. Our instinct is to keep cutting down trees instead of sharpening our axe. In other words, we really want to *feel* productive. And when we want to *feel* productive, we give in to something I've lovingly termed the job-search junk-food diet.

Job-search junk-food diet = an unhealthy lifestyle in which one effectively pushes (digital) paper around one's desk, for many unproductive hours a day, in the hope of finding work

How do you know if you're addicted to job-search junk-food? You know you're addicted if you sit at your desk for eight hours a day because you know you need to find a job and you *need* to be productive *right now today*. You scroll through 200 job postings — anything that you can find online — or maybe even 300, actually. You bookmark them, save them, organise them. You baulk at the ones that seem to have pretty complicated application processes. You can do those tomorrow. You have a 45-minute freak-out where you think maybe you *should* actually move to London. Then you remember you don't have the money to move to London. You put together one application, but you don't send it off. You'll do that tomorrow. And then, in hour number seven, you see one job posting that doesn't require a cover letter, and it's almost dinner time so you just shoot your CV off right then and there. (What was the name of that company? Can't remember. They'll email you if you get it anyway.)

And look at that! You can tell everyone you looked for work today without lying. You'll get through this day, and it will be exhausting and time-consuming, and even though you know that it probably wasn't the best way to go about it, you honestly didn't have any better ideas at the time and you needed so desperately to be productive *right now today*, because you need a new job *so badly*, and so you got through it in the only way you knew how.

Phew.

I know I've certainly done it this way. I spent years doing it this way, in fact. And 99% of job seekers will spend the next 30 years doing it this way, too — sometimes even after they have skills and connections in abundance. I don't ever want you to send in an application this way, ever again.

Why not? Because *you know the statistics*. You *know* how few people get hired through the 'front door' by sending in their CV to some info@ inbox without context. You *know* how much more likely it is for people to get hired — especially for the jobs you want

— through personal connections. Someday, over a glass of wine, we can sit and have a whole other conversation about the missteps and pitfalls of nepotism — but you still need a job *right now today*, remember? Luckily, I am going to teach you how to operate inside this system, even if you don't know the 'right' people.

We need to start by re-architecting the entire situation. We need to start by pouring a fresh slab of concrete and putting a hard ban on the endless scrolling of the job-search junk-food diet. Your new life does not begin with edits to your CV or cover letter templates, so don't skip ahead. It starts with writing down your hit list of target employers.

Be careful. Creating this list is deceptively simple. All you have to do is answer three questions:

What kind of role do you want?

Where are you physically going to get hired?

Which industry do you want to work in?

I cannot stress enough how important it is to have answers to these questions. On first glance, they seem easy to answer and tempting to skip over. Perhaps you just read through them without even pausing to reflect. Heed this word of warning from the Ghost of Employment Future: *If you do not lay down this foundation, you will get distracted almost immediately and quickly regress into your old job-search junk-food ways.* You will spend the next three months trying to chop down the opportunity tree with the strategic equivalent of a dull toothbrush.

Defining the ecosystem in which you want to work is easily the most important and strategic things you can (and should) get done today.

What kind of role do you want?

As we established with incorrect belief #1, I tend to lose my cool every time someone tells me they want a job in marketing (see page 5) because a 'job in marketing' narrows down your search results from 20 million to 4 million postings, tops.

If you know what you want — what you really, really want — then you need to say it out loud in the most specific terms possible. You don't want a job in business development, you want an entry-level sales role where you can nurture current partner relationships while learning how to pitch for new accounts from more senior managers. You don't just want a job in manufacturing, you want a sourcing job on the supply chain side, so that you can spend your days tracking down local organic linens for a sustainable pyjama brand.

I'm constantly surprised at how many job seekers skip this step. People aren't mind readers. No fairy godperson is going to look at your CV and think, 'Yes, yes! I know just the job for her! Quick, someone get me my employment paperwork!' You need to decide on what you want, so that you can articulate it to a total stranger over dinner. The more specific you can get about the types of skills you can bring to the table, the more easily someone else can understand whether or not you are needed by their organisation.

To illustrate, I'll tell you about this dinner party I attended once.

It was a half-social half-networking thing for a group of people who didn't know each other at all. About halfway through the meal, one woman mentioned that she was looking for a job. Before I could open my mouth, someone across the table popped the question, 'What are you looking for? Maybe one of us can help.'

What happened next was just magic. Without hesitation, she said, 'I'm looking for COO roles at 100–150-employee businesses, probably wrapping up their Series B funding. I'm not interested in joining a smaller company, I want the product to have validation already — and I'm more useful at later stages anyway. Ideally, it would be a company with a strong social change mission statement.'

Succinct. Specific. Empowered. Exact. Epic, if I'm being honest. If you can go into this level of detail about what you're looking for, whether you're in search of a day's worth of volunteer work or the role of a lifetime, you'll find you're a lot more unstoppable than you realise.

If you don't know exactly what kind of role you want, you need to do the work to figure it out step by step. You, too, need to get as specific as possible. If you're 100% straight out of school and have no idea what kind of career you want, go and start Googling your way towards the answer. Whenever you find a field that looks interesting, your next step is to find out as much as you can about it. Look for articles written on the topic, figure out if there's anybody in your own network who has that kind of job, start asking as many questions as possible. Try to dive deep and get curious, detective-style.

If you're not excited about your current role, and you're trying to pivot, try picking apart the aspects of your most recent position that you liked the most and building a new idea out of those pieces. For example, let's say your last role was 50% Task A, 20% Task B, and 30% Task C — and the part you liked the best was that one day a week when you got to do Task B stuff. You could start building your new job title around that task. (Who's going to stop you?)

Polly, a New Zealander now working in Germany, has a great story about gravitating towards the tasks you like and using that opportunity to make a bigger leap:

> I used to work in media planning for a TV channel, but no one was running the social media, so I took it on as a side project and dedicated about 20% of my week to it. It was doing so well that, when we got *New Zealand's Got Talent*

commissioned, I negotiated a half-day extra to dedicate to working on the show as the social media co-ordinator. From all this social media experience, I managed to move into a purely social media job at a bank and have only worked on social media ever since — my boring media planning job is a thing of the past. It was great to be able to switch so seamlessly between two totally different roles. At the time, I felt like my media planning job was so specialised that it would be hard to switch to anything more creative without taking a pay cut.

What we're trying to avoid here, from all directions, is a lack of clarity. You never want to make somebody guess what kind of position you might be right for, I promise you. The confused mind always says no. When I was early in my career, I thought I was being helpful when I just threw my CV into people's hands and asked them to let me know if there were any positions available that were 'suited' to my skillset.

As a hiring manager friend said to me once, 'Oh, yeah, sure. Let me take my entire day and try to match your skills to the 70 job descriptions on our Careers page and see what I can find for you. Don't worry, I have plenty of hours to spend on this for you.'

Nobody can read your mind. Nobody, frankly, has the time. The fastest way for you to get what you want is to name it out loud. You should constantly be banging the same drum, again and again, whenever you get the chance: 'These are my skills. This is the kind of job title I am planning to have for my next role. This is how I will help your team succeed. Do you want in on this, or not?'

TIP
If you're considering making a giant leap from one discipline to another and you require more information about your potential new career path, make use of the Magical Spark networking tactics in Step 8.

Where are you physically going to get hired?

We've been conditioned to believe that we must move to big cities, where the jobs are, and that we'll never find satisfying or stable work in a smaller town. We accept this as fact, but it's a fallacy, stemming from an antiquated line of thought. It's not 1959 anymore. It's not even 1999 anymore, for that matter. You don't have to move to London (or Cardiff or Newcastle or any other city) to get a great job.

There has always been a divide in the kinds of jobs you can access in different places, and it's not surprising that cities are seen as opportunity centres, with 'everywhere else' considered, well, a bit of a backwater. But this is no longer the case for many industries. The internet has levelled the geographical playing field, and will continue to do so, more and more, with each year that passes. In particular, if a company has a service or product to promote online and deliver from afar, the internet offers the possibility of doing that from absolutely anywhere. What that means for you, job seeker, is that there may be several dozen (and possibly several hundred) rapidly growing businesses that are hiring right now in your own back garden, or wherever you want your back garden to be.

I really want you to soak this in. It's simultaneously revolutionary and liberating. You do not have to leave Nottingham or Cologne or Hobart if you don't want to. You can build an awesome career, with a lower cost of living, from a variety of smaller markets. So, if you want to stay where you are, do that. And if your heart is screaming for New York or London or Milan or whatever, you can do that, too. There is no wrong answer and, crucially, there's a less restricted path than there used to be.

Do not let anybody give you out-of-date facts about the job market in your city. Do your own research.

PAUSE

Do you feel like you have permission to go to (or stay in) a place you didn't think you were allowed to build a life in? Did you need that permission? If so, sit with it for a moment.

'Oh, I'd go anywhere.'

There's another strain of bad geographical advice which you might have soaked in somewhere along the way: to not be fussy about where you work. 'Go to where the jobs are,' we've been told. 'You can't be too choosy if you get a good opportunity.'

It's well intentioned, and it kind of makes sense. You should want to be hungry, flexible, and ready to move mountains for a promising new role. Those are good instincts that stem from a strong work ethic and core values. The 'go anywhere' mentality, however, often results in more missed opportunities than gained ones. Take this benign conversation you might have with a family friend as an example:

You: I'm looking for a new job right now, actually!
Family friend: Oh great, I'm sure I know some people who are hiring. You want to stay in Manchester, right?
You: I'll go anywhere.
Family friend: Oh, okay. So, not Manchester?
You: I'm considering Manchester, but I'm thinking about moving to London or maybe even Melbourne.
Family friend: Wow, how great! Good luck! *(Gosh, I always wanted to go to Melbourne. I'm not going to introduce them to my friend Jane who's hiring in Manchester, it sounds like they've got exciting plans!)*

So, in order to successfully complete the Step 1 exercises, you need to pick one place.

Throughout this whole process, I'm often going to encourage you to narrow things down instead of expanding them. It will feel counter-intuitive for a while, when the adrenaline in your veins is screaming 'I would take any job, anywhere, right now!' and begging you to send out another half-baked application. That's your old mentality talking, clinging to the job-search junk-food diet for the sake of feigning momentum.

There's an important, hidden benefit to narrowing your job search radius. A single place inherently offers up an interconnected community of professionals, many of whom have worked with more than one employer over the course of their careers. Interconnectivity offers the possibility of referrals within the network, even when you're just starting out. I will teach you everything you need to know about networking when we get there. For now, this geographic focus sets us up with a solid foundation for that networking. (And if you need to stay in a specific place, for family or for health or for whatever, this makes your life easy! This constraint is a good thing.)

I know it can all sound a little *Oh! The Places You'll Go* before you've even started. You will meet a lot of people along your job search journey who may not be able to hire you personally — but they absolutely know someone who can. And due to the migration patterns of the average human, people in Birmingham tend to mostly know people in Birmingham. It's far less likely that someone in Leeds can help you get a job in Bristol, or that somebody in Adelaide can help you get a job in Auckland. This will slowly change with the internet, but we aren't there quite yet. Don't discount how important this kind of geographic interconnectivity is to the future of your career.

So, for today, we pick a place. If you must, you can pick a different one tomorrow. Take this as a first opportunity to release the pressure gasket on your search. Luxuriate in the clarity of specificity, my friend.

Which industry do you want to work in?

There's a critical distinction to be made between choosing an industry and choosing a department or role. We are gravitationally drawn towards having an existential crisis about our current or future job title, when there are sometimes bigger fish to fry. Our career 'specialties' — the kinds of roles we want, such as marketing or accounting, which we looked at in question 1 — are almost exclusively skills-focused. This is ingrained into the way that we're taught at school, the degrees that we hold, and the way we're advised to focus our professional interest areas. *A degree in computer science. A BTEC in business studies. An apprenticeship in social work.* All of these are just skillsets or broad expertise areas that you're meant to use for a bigger purpose: to sell or run or create or organise or support or streamline or bring awareness to *something else.*

Here's another way to put it: if you're in operations, what are you organising? If you're an accountant, what kind of things are you counting? If you're in communications, what do you want to communicate about? If you're a data analyst, what are you analysing?

I was hell-bent on getting an internship in public relations during my university term abroad in London. An internship meant I could take one less class, and it provided the added benefit of hopefully meeting Real Live British People out in the wild. I scored a PR internship, just like I wanted. At the end of those four months, however I don't remember learning *that* much about the nuanced art of public relations. I do remember learning *a ton* about modern European furniture designers. Thonet chairs? I could tell you all about their German heritage. Norwegian lamp designers? I knew the up-and-coming names on the scene. I learned all of this because, without really putting too much thought into it, I had signed on to do an internship with a boutique PR agency that specialised exclusively in contemporary European interiors.

Luckily, I happen to love contemporary European interiors. So chic.

The end of that internship is when it clicked for me. If you don't care about the thing you're talking about all day long — which was expensive furniture, not PR itself — you're going to have a hard time motivating yourself to put your skills to work day in and day out. When you're specialising in public relations, your entire job is to get other people to love whatever you're publicising — in this case, modern European furniture. Those chairs are what you're drumming up publicity for on a consistent basis.

In other words, it's not about having a job in marketing. It's about *what* you're marketing.

Do you want to market luxury hotels? Do you want to market the tourism industry in Turkey? Do you want to market ocean-front seafood restaurants in Hawaii? Do you have a passion for fluffy bathrobes and organic linen pillowcases? Congratulations, you probably want to work in the travel and hospitality industry.

> **PAUSE**
> If you don't have an immediate answer to the industry question, pause and think about it for a while. As with choosing a place, it's actually less helpful if your answer is 'any industry'.

When I was looking for my first full-time job, I subconsciously limited myself to all the 'professional' industries I could name: large corporate retailers, consumer packaged-goods manufacturers, corporate consulting, and giant media agency conglomerates. I assumed that the only companies with good jobs were the ones with serious-looking websites that did or sold Very Grown-up Things. I focused on these giant corporations — companies that were so big, I could hardly even tell you what they did — because

I figured the bigger the company, the more jobs they'd have open for somebody like me. It was the wrong approach. I couldn't bring myself to get excited about starting my career at any of these places. All the jobs sounded boring, even if they would have been a great fit for somebody else. Because of my low interest levels, I was shooting myself in the foot.

I was experiencing a common career pitfall. I avoided the industries I was actually interested in — Music! Fashion! Content production! — for the same reason that so many of us do. We've been told time and again that they're hard to crack. We are usually told this by people who have never worked in these industries. We are told that it's too complicated and too hard, and so we give up before ever exploring it for ourselves. I implore you: do not do this.

If there's an industry you're really excited about, just go take your shot. This is your time to make it happen for yourself. When you undoubtedly get told that it's hard to get into the industry, I want you to repeat the following mantra: *Why not me? I'm smart. I'm sure they need more help from smart, passionate people.*

The cool industries have reputations for a reason. Because they're popular and fun-sounding, a lot of people are interested in trying to get a job simply because they (stupidly) assume their life will be all parties, glamour, travel, and sleepovers.

It won't be, and you know that. You have all the skills you need to crack the industry of your choice because you've made the decision to be thoughtful, disciplined, and strategic about your job search. At the end of the day, even the very coolest-of-cool industries are still just multi-billion-dollar machines that need smart people to help them grow. Just think about how many thousands of people all over the world have gone before you, successfully managing to get hired in music or fashion. *Every* multi-billion-dollar industry needs people to make it work. None of these industries is too full for new talent. They never will be.

Where to start if you don't know where to start

- **Make a list of all the industries that you find interesting.**
  If you really can't get excited about anything, start with the
  most extreme industries you can dream up. Gin. Luxury
  watches. Summer camps. Ethically produced lingerie. Pet
  grooming. Social media influencers. Viral video production
  … Your turn, keep listing them.

- **Spend all of tomorrow tracking the ways in which you
  spend your own time.** Are you constantly playing video
  games? Addicted to online shoe shopping? Which games?
  Which brands? Which websites? Write them down.

- **Think about what you eat or use during the day.** Do you
  have a specific snack you eat religiously at 3pm every day?
  Are you obsessed with your pillowcase? Can you even get
  out of bed without coffee? Okay, coffee from where? Figure
  out who the suppliers and manufacturers are for all of these
  products and services.

If you don't feel that strongly about a specific place, get curious
about where some cool companies from your dream industry are
located and work backwards. If you've already got a specific place
in mind, don't assume you know everything that's going on there.
You'd be surprised to learn about the random businesses that are
headquartered in random places around the world.

Please, please, please do not pass Go until you have answers to all three of these questions. You are going to be amazed at the clarity you'll feel once you can confidently look yourself in the mirror and say, 'I am looking for a social media coordinator role in the fashion industry in Liverpool.'

By stringing together this one single sentence, your job search instantly crystallises into something tangible. Anyone who knows where they want to work and in which industry is lightyears ahead of the pack, because it is exponentially easier to provide help, networking connections, and job leads to one of these two people:

Person 1: I am looking for a social media coordinator role in the fashion industry in Liverpool.
Person 2: I am looking for a job in marketing.

Can you see the difference? The fashion industry in Liverpool is a defined search zone. There exists a finite number of employers within that space, and that's a very good thing. What's even better? The people working on the inside of that defined search zone are likely all connected in some way. Maybe they worked together at a previous employer. Maybe two competitors are secretly plotting to start a new company. If you get in good with one employer, it will be that much easier to get hired at the next. Even if Company 1 has no vacancies, they likely know who to refer you to at Company 2 or 3.

Setting these parameters sets you up for success, in both the shortterm and the longterm. The dominoes fall swiftly once you put your constraints in place. Here are some examples to inspire you:

• I am looking for a legal assistant role on the rights and acquisitions team for a top-tier streaming service (Netflix, HBO, Amazon or similar). I am based in London.

- I am looking for a purchasing and supply chain role in the commercial construction industry in Singapore.
- I am looking for an early childhood educator position at a museum or art gallery in Glasgow.
- I am looking for a junior or apprentice brewer job at a craft beer brewery in New South Wales.

Your mission now is to make yourself a list with the details for 10–15 employers who have offices in the place you want to live in, who are connected to the industry you want to work in. (If you also need to get more specific about which kind of roles you're going for, start to put in that work, too.)

Train your focus. Put on your blinders. Write down the names of real companies and organisations. This should take you an entire day, if not two or three. It's a full-fledged research assignment. Take all that time you would have spent bookmarking jobs you look vaguely qualified for, and do this instead.

This list is your nutritional plan to combat the job-search junk-food diet. No more applying to 5,000 jobs a day. No more skimming for keywords on LinkedIn. Quiet down the noise and block out the distractions. You're about to write the name of your future employer down on this list. And if you hold in your hands a list that names your future employer, you don't need to spend another day scrolling through the internet looking at jobs you don't even want, do you? Distraction is Enemy Number One, and this list is your weapon for combatting that enemy.

What to collect for every target employer

1. Name of company, of course
2. Position open OR position wanted
3. A few employee contacts to hit up later

Name of company

The job-search junk-food diet has trained us to prioritise looking for open roles over interesting employers. Stop just looking at sales assistant role after sales assistant role and letting the employer take a backseat to whether or not you meet enough of the requirements listed on the page in front of you.

I demand that you flip these two back into place and re-establish a better hierarchy.

Whether you went to university or not, think about how the application process works. Potential students don't just apply to the English department, they apply to the institution itself. It would sound ridiculous if your application strategy was to hastily throw together an application for every single university in the country that happened to have an English department. There's so much more to consider: where is the campus? Does the culture fit you? Do you agree with the university's values? (Yes, you have to apply to the English department, too, but you usually don't do it without even knowing where the university is!)

Creating a list of target employers trains your brain to follow a similar model.

Position open/position wanted

There's one trap to look out for with this new system, and that's the concept of an open position. We already explored why the online job posting system is equal parts valuable and fallible (see page 26), and that holds true when you're putting together your Target

Employer List. It's extremely possible that an employer on this list has a possible vacancy about to come online in the very near future, even if there's nothing listed on their website.

- **What to do if there's a position listed that looks right for you:** Write it down. You'll want to prioritise chasing down these employers — because if you can see that job posting, so can everybody else.
- **What to do if there's no position listed that looks right for you:** Turn on your detective mode, and try to track down the person(s) with the role most similar to the role that you would want.

The positions listed on a company's Careers page (if they even have one) are usually only the tip of the iceberg. There might be so many other positions that are just about to open up. Someone's contract is about to end. Someone is about to quit. Someone is trying to build a case to their boss for why they need to hire some help. Your dream employment situation will require you to do some digging around. It's a worthwhile pursuit.

Employee contacts to hit up

Gathering the names of *employers* should be your primary focus before all else. These last suggestions are for collecting useful information that you find along the way, so that you don't have to retrace your steps again later on.

Example: You come across an employer you're really excited about, but they don't have any vacancies listed. You can, however, see online that they currently employ two marketing assistants — and that's exactly the kind of job you want to snag. Write both of their names down.

Example: During your mini-research session on an interesting employers, you read on the company's About page that someone on their team went to the same school you did. I know, how random. Write that person's name down.

Don't worry about reaching out yet. We'll get there. For now, we're just collecting information.

Step 1 task list

1. Decide to focus — even just for practice — on one industry that is really calling to you. You can keep it broad (like 'hospitality') or you can narrow it down (like 'sustainable women's fashion e-retailers').
2. Find 10–15 companies that do business within your chosen industry *and* within your chosen city. Google your way through it. If you are not planning on moving to Miami, do not look at jobs in Miami. Life is too short, and we have too much to do.
3. Take 15 minutes (per employer) to look up their job postings *and* look through employee profiles you can find online. Some employers list team members on their About page. You can also type the company name into the search bar on LinkedIn. Click on 'People who work at [Company Name]' and you should see a list of employee profiles. From here on out, start collecting people intel whenever you see it.
4. For each employer, find 1–2 jobs (that you see posted *or* that you see on LinkedIn) that look like a good fit. For our purpose, these should be within reach — so look for postings that roughly match your current skillset OR that you seem to have at least 50% of the right skills for already.

Remember, this is the biggest homework assignment you'll have for the rest of the job search, because it will lay a rock-solid foundation for your search. It's a time-consuming project. It will be so worth it. Take a week and really get this one right.

Step 2: Hack your own skillset

'I really want to learn to paddleboard,' I said absent mindedly, looking out at the ocean from my seat on the train from San Diego to Los Angeles.

'What's there to learn?' my friend replied, not looking up from his magazine. 'You get a board. You drag the board into the ocean. You stand up. You paddle.'

I went red. What did I think the board was going to do, sneak up and murder me while I ungracefully tried to paddle around in very calm waters? What kind of supervision did I think this required? He was right, of course. Yes, I could theoretically learn to paddleboard by paying for a class. Some surfing shop would definitely take my money, ensure that a lifeguard was on duty, have me sign an insurance waiver form, and make me practise standing up in the sand while someone with more upper-body strength than I could ever dream of dragged the board into the ocean on my behalf. It had never have occurred to me that I could just rent a board and see what happened. This friend, on the other hand, had always been a natural athlete. I'd watched once, from the safety of a lounge chair in the Dominican Republic, while he went out into the ocean alone and repeatedly wrestled a windsurfing board into the waves. He knew he could teach himself — and that's exactly what Step 2 is asking of you.

Your mission: Proactively go 1. identify, 2. prioritise, and 3. teach yourself a skill that will make you more hireable in your chosen line of work. You must do this in parallel to your job search. You must put in the hours to become more hireable *while you also* put in the hours to go get hired. (Now you've quit the job-search junk-food diet and no longer spend your time scrolling through job postings all night long, you definitely have the time to go and learn something new.)

Whether you start hacking your current position so that you're upskilling for the next role, or whether you're still in school or university or unemployed and don't know what else to do with those extra hours in your day: learn!

Here's the thing: we waste months — years, even — searching for jobs that match our current skillsets. This is the accepted norm. We wait for a job to appear, because we were promised that our education 'qualifies' us for some kind of work — and that, if we can't find work, we should go straight back into the classroom for another qualification. We wait because we were told that, so long as we're hard-working once we manage to get the job, it will be enough. We sit and rest on our hard-won academic laurels, or we rely on the skills we picked up in our last position. We wait. We only look at job postings for positions we might be 'qualified' for, as if our qualifications are a thing over which we have no control. We play mental Twister while we look through job requirements, cancelling ourselves out of the game as soon as we deem ourselves unfit for duty. *Skills Red, Yellow, Blue — check, check, check! Oh, shoot. Green. No. Nothing I can do about it, eh? On to the next job posting.*

Too many of us were taught that the only two ways to acquire new skills are 1. by enrolling in an 'official' academic program, or 2. by receiving training in a paid full-time job. This belief will fail you. It will ruin you. It will be the reason you never make the leap from where you are now to where you hope you're headed next.

The deeper we get into the 21st century, the faster you need to get on board with the teach-yourself mentality. Knowledge is out there and it's yours for the taking. The internet generation, for all its woes, has been afforded an unprecedented opportunity: access to information. The idea that you need to wait around for permission before you educate yourself on a topic predates the Third Industrial Revolution (AKA the economic shift prompted by the rise of the 'personal computer' that began, by the way, back in the mid-1980s, before I was even born). We're at this interesting point at which degrees and qualifications are still spoken about in the same way they were pre-internet, but that narrative simply isn't true anymore. Reality is shifting — has shifted — faster than you might think.

Whenever you need to upskill yourself for employment, you can just … go do it.

Heather McGowan, a future of work strategist who helps companies and educational institutions adapt to this new reality, summarised the situation beautifully for me:

> We are coming out of an era that my colleague Chris Shipley and I call the learn-to-work era. In that era, the promise was that, if you learned once, particularly by achieving an undergraduate degree, you could work the rest of your life in relatively stable comfort. Now the velocity of change is such that all your technical skills have a shelf life of about five years. You will now have to work to learn, continuously, to adapt to the evolving nature of work. Degrees are great, but that is the starting point. 'Educated' used to be end-state, which credentialed you to the necessary standards in order to 'qualify' for a job. In a hyperconnected and interdependent global economy, stored knowledge expires quickly.

It's equal parts scary and exciting, right? A lack of education is no longer a permanent jail sentence, but rather a puzzle to go out and solve. Not to go full Oprah on you, but you have the permission and the power to change the trajectory of your career and your life any time you like, including in the middle of this very job search.

Every single skill you might want to add to your toolbelt — whether that's a mastery of a specific accounting software or a better understanding of people management and employee retention — is available to you outside of the academic environment. You have access to this information on the internet, right now, often for free or at a very low price-point. Incredibly talented educators — on YouTube, Skillshare, Udemy, LinkedIn Learning, and more — are at your fingertips.

A little bit of clever Googling will reveal them to you.

If you've yet to try learning something new on the internet, I think you'll be surprised at the quality and variety of educational styles you can find. I spoke at length about the digital learning world with Ryan Holdaway, the VP of outcomes for Lambda School. (Lambda is a fast-growing online school, where you can learn in-demand digital skills for free and only pay back the tuition *after* you get a job.) He pointed out this key perk of our new reality:

> One of the most important things we've learned is that people learn at different rates and through different ways. The internet makes it a lot easier to learn in a way that's best for you. If traditional education isn't your thing, try out an online course. If online courses aren't your thing, use the internet to meet a mentor, or simply utilise a gig economy site in order to test-drive the job you want and build your portfolio. There are myriad ways to get new skills that don't involve spending the next four years in a physical classroom.

What about all those degrees that you already paid for and the qualifications you already have, you might be wondering? No idea. Some of them will be valuable, and some of them won't be worth as much as you had hoped. I won't begrudge you a day's worth of moaning about how the modern education system has failed us. If you're already sitting on a ticking time bomb of student debt and wondering if all that money was even worth it, seeing as you're apparently just having to keep teaching yourself new stuff all the time, I hear you. I see you. I am angry for you.

But while I give you permission to get frustrated for a day or two, I do not give you permission to simply throw in the towel. If your whole career strategy is to wait for someone else to solve insanely complex societal problems, you will be waiting for a very long time. Your rent is still due no matter what, remember? So, we keep going.

Go. Get curious, again and again and again. Get curious about your desired career move, even if you think you already have the skills needed. There's always something new to learn or new to brush up on. If you want to be hired and treated as one of the best-of-the-best in your industry, you've got to act like it. As McGowan explained to me, 'We have only digitised about 20% of our economy, so the greatest waves of change have yet to hit us. Hacking your skills is necessary for continuous adaptation. Those with learning agility will best adapt and thrive.'

(That, and learning how to constantly reshape your narrative and pitch your skillset. That's the part you're learning about in this book!)

QUICK CLARIFICATION

Specialists that require academic or vocational training that can only legally be recognised by official bodies, please ignore me. If you need to get a degree or a specific qualification in order to legally be allowed to do your job, keep on keeping on. You know who you are. But if you were just hoping that a Vague Degree might make you a more attractive candidate for Some Kind of Job, do heed this advice.

Identifying teeny-tiny skills

These new things you're going to go out and learn: they can (and should) be small, specific skills. I've worked with a lot of students who think the skills they already have aren't good enough, and their instinct is to overcorrect. They frantically overcompensate by writing down a comically massive homework assignment like 'learn Mandarin' or 'learn SEO' or 'learn coding'. While I'm all for big ambitions, I have to stop you there. We need to crack this open. Coding is a great example to use here due to its popularity and complexity.

1. **Do you *want* to code, day in and day out?** If yes, sweet, let's make it happen. If not, that's okay. Coding (or whatever skill) is not the only way you're going to find a job. Please don't choose a skill you think you 'should' learn but are only writing down to make somebody else happy or because you think it's the 'right' answer. As a reference point, by the way, most people would need five to seven months of basically full-time training in order to 'code' at a hireable level.

2. **Can you get more specific?** I'll continue with the coding example. 'Coding' means at least a dozen different things, so I will challenge you to dig deeper here. When you say 'coding', do you mean …

   – Back-end development?
   – Front-end development?
   – Data engineering? SQL?
   – Visual UI design?
   – Statistical data modelling?
   – Developing A/B tests for conversion?

–   Brushing up on HTML/WordPress for content
     management?

If you have no idea what I'm talking about, that's kind of my
point. When you say something like 'coding' or 'fundraising' or
'leadership' or 'SEO' or 'digital marketing', you are using a broad
umbrella term that encompasses so many skills, it might as well be
meaningless. I want you to pick something that feels *really specific*.
That's the thing to go learn about in a deeper way.

At most companies, multiple people are tackling that thing
you might currently be referring to as one single 'skill'. Get curious
about that. Do a little Googling. Trawl through job descriptions.
If you see a skill mentioned that you don't understand, research it.
Approach this like a puzzle.

A few quick-fire skill-hacking ideas

Problem: You want to be the next celebrity florist, but you've been rejected from every floristry job you've applied for so far.
Solution: Find ways to build a stronger portfolio. Ask to shadow a wedding planner or interior designer in your city. Design the centrepieces for a local school fundraiser. Boom — you just increased your 'Hire Me!' factor tenfold.

Problem: You are ready to get hired as a team lead or as a manager, but you don't have anybody who reports to you directly and you don't know how to prove you're ready for the challenge.
Solution: Create your own opportunity to demonstrate your leadership potential by going beyond the scope of your core job. Pilot an internal programme in your office. Volunteer to lead the company-wide charity effort. Prove that you can manage by finding something to manage, and managing it.

Problem: You want to get into tech, but you didn't study computer science at university.
Solution: Spend a day researching what you mean by 'tech', and if the positions you want actually require software development knowledge. Never assume you know which skills are required for a job. If you do need to learn, Google around until you find an online class. Look up hackathons in your city and spend your Saturday asking the people you meet there for recommendations.

A very incomplete list of times I have hacked my own skillset

1. In my second-ever internship, I made some tagline suggestions for an advertisement that I was collecting from the art director's desk. The head of the marketing department asked me if I would start writing all the taglines for similar advertise-

ments in the future, and if I would be interested in continuing to do so (remotely) for the rest of the year. I said yes. That was the accidental start of my freelance copywriting career.

2. My first experience with social media marketing was when I wanted to promote my own recitals during my Master's degree. I wasn't necessarily that good at it, but when I was later asked in interviews if I knew how to set up and run a Facebook page, I could say, 'Yep.'

3. One summer when I was underemployed with freelance work, I became the unpaid Chief Marketing Officer of a Berlin-based fashion company. We shot a brand video to use on the website on a Saturday morning. I sat and fed questions to the CEO while she was in front of the camera, helping her work through her lines over multiple takes. At the end, I thought, *Huh. I guess I know a little bit about how to produce video content now.*

4. In 2015, I decided to run my own small crowdfunding campaign to raise the funds I needed to record a new album. After I successfully hit my target, I was approached by a couple of copywriting clients of mine who wanted to know if I would consider joining their team full-time for three to six months, so that I could run *their* crowdfunding campaigns. I could have used that moment to intentionally pivot my career if I had wanted to, just because of a personal project.

IMPORTANT

You'll notice a pattern with my particular brand of hacking. Sometimes, you actually already have the skills you need — but you have decided they aren't allowed to 'count' because you weren't in education or getting paid (see: volunteering, hobbies, religious service, family responsibilities). But those skills *do* count. As I said to you early on, the top skill you need is the ability to explain why the skills you already have are valuable.

Some really good advice from gainfully employed people

Over the course of writing this book, I spoke to hundreds of people about how they started their own careers. Everyone lit up when it came to the topic of learning new skills on the fly. I consolidated some of the best advice I heard …

If you find yourself constantly having to ask someone to do something for you, teach yourself that skill. Google and YouTube have countless free tutorials that are easy to follow — just pick something and give it a try! I graduated with a degree in Psychology and another in Sociology. I taught (am constantly teaching) myself coding in Excel/Google Sheets that allows me to more easily keep up with a large volume of contacts and individual checklists, and I have gotten proficient enough in basic graphic design that I am able to do a lot of my own social media stuff in-house.

Jake, director of admissions and PR for a high school,
American, living in Detroit

When learning to produce music, I picked one song ('Lucky' by Britney Spears) and recreated it as closely as possible. Not only in its original style, but in a variety of different styles (more indie, more dance-y, etc). I probably made 12–15 versions of the song, and though there was nothing 'useable' in any of them, it was an incredibly quick way to absorb the essentials of production. This can be applied to almost anything. To learn Mandarin, I watched *The Matrix* (Mandarin audio, English subtitles, which I phased out after week four) two to four times per day for eight months. If you're the obsessive type, use it and dive in. Pick one thing in the field you can easily lose yourself in, and get lost.

Crook, freelance songwriter and music producer,
Irish, living in Berlin

When most people think of skills, they jump to academic degrees (see: MBA in Finance) or actions to perform (see: how to use Adobe InDesign). Some of the most important and in-demand 'skills' are, instead, very useful subsets of knowledge based on experience and research. Most of these 'skills' aren't taught in schools; but rather, are learned in real-world scenarios mixed with a healthy amount of Googling. Off the top of my head, here are some examples of knowledge areas that are desperately needed:

GDPR compliance (What is GDPR? How do companies become compliant?)

Recruiting (How do innovative brands connect to candidates? What do great interview processes look like for your industry's most popular employers and how much would it cost for a competitor to do the same?)

Legal (How are Master Service Agreements generally structured? What's an indemnification clause?)

Cailey, director of finance at a software company,
American, living in Atlanta

Being on the inside gives you the opportunity to identify gaps that you could fill! My degree was in Pre-Medicine and Theology. I only applied for my first job because I ran out of graduation money and the listing said 'Recent graduates accepted'. The job was for a medical-record software implementation analyst at a hospital. Even though I had taken zero computer science classes, I made a conscious effort to become a valuable member of the team and a resource for new team members. Since then, I've been able to transition onto different teams, allowing me to continually build my skillset in different areas! (And as for my degree, I've used my theology degree more than my pre-med degree since graduation … I taught third-grade catechism for two years!)

Hannah, advanced analytics director for a healthcare company, American, living in New Orleans

Identify in-demand skills by looking at technology-based roles that haven't been around for very long: product manager, data scientist, growth marketer, user experience designer, for example. Start by finding experts in the discipline. Read their blog posts and follow them on Twitter. Interview them if you can. Find out the most influential resources they'd recommend. Read the top three to five important books on your chosen topic. Synthesise. Then, commit to teaching a small workshop. You can do this in person at a co-working space or online via webinar or live stream. If you're afraid that you aren't an expert on the topic, that's okay. The goal is to become an expert quickly, and there's no better way to do that than to force yourself to teach a topic. It's also a great way to get leads for jobs, as some of the people you'll end up teaching will need someone with exactly your new skillset.

Mattan, engineering professor for Columbia University's MBA Program, American, living in New York City

If you want to work in a particular industry but don't have the qualifications, get a temping job in that industry, and build up your knowledge and contacts. The number of temps I've seen become journalists without the qualifications, or

TV presenters or book editors. If you're smart, enthusiastic, and willing to work as a team, that counts for more than a degree or qualifications in a subject. And even if you need to go and train, then you have a much better understanding and contact base to walk into a great job when you get the qualifications you think you need.

Lucy, former video journalist at Associated Press,
British, living in London

Try breaking down all the skills you need to learn and the experiences/certifications you need to get into a list. How can you start checking things off that list now, without having to sign up for a full degree? For instance, if you need to learn financial analysis skills, can you take a course, find a local professional to mentor you, borrow a book from your library, or create your project using data from the internet? Often, working on your own will help you learn far faster than a classroom environment, because you have to learn how to solve problems quickly and independently. If you're interested in going back to education for the structure and guidance it will provide you, think about ways to create that for yourself. Maybe you make friends with someone else at your current job that also wants to learn new skills, and you both study together after work.

Katy, content strategist for a social media platform,
American, living in San Francisco

After university, I wanted to work in publishing, but I'd heard it was a competitive industry that relied on doing a lot of internships. I got a job running a local youth club while I tried to figure out my next steps. At work, I put my hand up for tasks that involved writing, editing, or print production, like putting together copy, flyers, and brochures, and along the way I taught myself how to use Adobe InDesign as I'd heard was industry standard software in publishing. I started applying for work experience with publishers and eventually one offered me a two-week placement. I loved it, and when my contract at the charity ended, I applied for more roles in publishing. The first question at one interview was whether I knew how to use InDesign! I said yes, and that wound up being my first job in the industry. I didn't have to pay for extra schooling or take courses outside of work.

Sarah, working in publishing, British, living in Melbourne

At my previous job I was hired for marketing, but I wanted to work on product design. Our CEO was the one doing all the designs. I gave him a mini-speech about how he could trust me, and then I spent the weekend learning how to wireframe. I learned by doing things outside of my job description — and, through that, learned what type of work I enjoy. I wasn't paid very well at that job, but in a year I got all the skills I needed and I didn't have to pay for extra schooling or take courses outside of work.

Denisse, content strategist for a social media platform,
American, living in San Francisco

Thoughts on working 'for free'

There is a big difference between finding a creative way to learn the skills you need and being asked to work for free when you already possess those skills. Doing the flowers for a fundraiser in order to start your own portfolio? Creative skill-building. Working for a florist for free when you already have a strong portfolio? Not so much.

Every industry has different 'norms' when it comes to unpaid work at the beginning of your career, not all of which are fair and equitable. In some of the more notorious industries, there are many wonderful activists pushing for stricter regulation around unpaid internships. But if you are waiting around for that first 'real' job that hires you 100% based on your potential and then provides you with a great training programme, please know that those opportunities are few and far between.

All I can tell you is that you need to set your own boundaries and that you should aim to start getting paid as quickly as possible once you cross the threshold into hireability. In this context, I'll define 'hireability' as being able to really, truly, skilfully do a job that you know someone else is getting paid to do.

I've heard more than one success story from someone who pitched their now-employer on the idea of a 'free trial month' to prove that they knew their stuff — and not just at junior levels in their careers, either. If you're in a position to sweeten the deal like this in order to get your foot in the door, go for it. You may wind up getting hired faster than you would have if the employer had gone away for a month to deliberate about which candidate they wanted to hire. What I really like about this is that it's a time-boxed offer. *I can give you a month, and then you decide. Otherwise, I'm moving on.*

I know that working full-time for free for an entire month isn't an opportunity everybody can afford (and really isn't necessary for every kind of job!). But I bring it up to remind you that there's always a creative way to get your foot in the door.

Use your time strategically. Take a night class, volunteer for a weekend, or use your lunch break to hone a specific skill. If you need a company or organisation to 'practise' on, I recommend trying to cut your teeth on a good cause. Your local schools, charities, places of worship, and small businesses could really use the help; and, because they could use the help, they're more likely to let you quickly jump in and get to work. The faster you can build skills, the faster you can put them on your CV and keep growing your career.

Where to start if you don't know where to start

This go-teach-yourself stuff may sound cheesy — or even obvious — once you see it all spelled it out like this, but 99% of people will still not take this advice. They won't go out and do it. I want you to write this down, post it up on your mirror, and repeat every day of your job search: *Be the one who goes out and does it.*

Go back through some of the job descriptions you already looked at during Step 1. Trawl through their skills or listed requirements, and start breaking these down. Make a list in three columns: 1. the skills you definitely have, 2. the skills you sort of have but you could improve, 3. the skills you don't know at all yet but are interested to learn more about.

Focus on that middle column first. The low-hanging fruit will be to move those skills into the 'definitely have' list. From there, create a priority order for the skills you don't have yet, so you can start slowly knocking them out.

> **IMPORTANT**
>
> Nobody is going to stop and frisk you in an interview someday, demanding to know where you obtained your skills. It absolutely does not matter if your skills are from a 'real' job or from a side project or from a charity or from freelancing or from a degree programme or from an online boot camp or from YouTube. If you develop skills in your own time, you get to claim those skills on your CV. You should be shouting about them, in fact. Look at you taking initiative!

Step 2 task list

1. **Identify where your current skillset comes up short based on which kinds of jobs you want to get hired for next.** Get as specific as possible. Draw inspiration from job descriptions.
2. **Create three tangible, actionable homework assignments for yourself.** That could be attending a local lecture, signing up for a night/online class, or just sitting down every night this week to write fake advertising slogans for Smirnoff Ice. Any way you slice it, it's all up to you.

Step 3: How to write the perfect CV

As you will certainly have realised by now, there's a reason this isn't the first chapter of the book. So, if you skipped ahead, go back. Ask the others if you don't believe me. *You are doing it wrong.*

The CV, while important, is not the *pièce de résistance* we make it out to be. For as long as I've been billing myself as a career coach, and for long before that, people have been coming to me for CV editing help. These people come to me in a frenzy, desperately seeking ... I don't know, some single PDF attachment to rule them all?

Friend, your job search success hangs on so much more than a single email attachment. I know how tempting it can be to treat your CV as a permanent record of your accomplishments, but it's actually a lot more fluid than that. Your CV is nothing more than an ever-changing sales pitch, tailored to one specific employer at a time. Similarly to how you'd think to tweak your opening pickup line at the bar a little bit for every individual, you need to learn to tweak your CV for every employer you approach. You are the only one who controls your professional narrative, and you get to reserve the right to change how you talk about your skills and career history at any time. Your skillset changes over the years, and so will the ways in which you connect the dots about your previous employers. How you explained yourself on a CV last year might not make sense anymore. I promise you, no one is going to submit you to a lie-detector test and demand to see a transcript of everything you did at every previous role you ever held. Your future employer simply wants to understand a few highlights, and why those particular highlights are relevant.

What I can offer you: a narrative structure that should help you to highlight your talents effectively. Great copywriting tips. Ways to stand out. Proven techniques for painting the clearest possible picture of you and your strengths.

WHO WILL THIS CV FORMAT WORK FOR?

Meh, everybody-ish. While this format will work like a charm for those with four or more years of experience, it was explicitly designed to also work well for those who have only had internships or part-time jobs so far. And if you're even more junior than that — perhaps you haven't left school yet and you're applying for your first Saturday job or internship ever! — you can exchange the Experience section for a Leadership & Activities section. The way you should speak about your relevant experience should remain the same, whether you're talking about a salaried role or a student government position. If you are nervous about whether or not your official work experience is 'good enough', please give this a chance.

When writing a CV, I always want you to be thinking about ...

- **What to highlight, and what to skim over.** Your CV can and should look different based on the specifics of that position. You don't have to list every single thing you did at every position. If Projects A and B are more relevant for the role, give them prime real estate. On the next CV, you might highlight Projects B and C instead. You don't even have to put everything on a CV. Again: think sales pitch, not permanent record.

- **How you can position volunteer work, unpaid extracurriculars, or self-taught skills.** As we just spoke about in Step 2, all experience is legitimate, and you get to decide what's relevant. Just because you weren't on the payroll doesn't mean you don't get to 'count' what you learned or how you contributed. For the rest of your working life, your most valuable weapon will be the ability to understand and articulate why the experiences you had in one job are transferable to another. You get to start using that weapon right now, today.

My first portfolio featured, almost exclusively, work that 'shouldn't count'. I was trying to score a junior social media management job, and the person who ultimately became my boss asked me if I had any experience running social media accounts. 'I run my own Facebook page, actually,' I said in our initial meeting. 'I mean, it's a really tiny project, it's just for my music. I use it to promote my gigs, tell people about my new recordings, stuff like that.'

To my amazement, he said that sounded great and wanted to see examples. I went home, screenshotted the best of those Facebook posts, and put them up online next to the few pieces of work that I had to show from my one 'legitimate' internship. I screenshotted a couple of posts from my Twitter and my SoundCloud that felt relevant, too. I got the job.

Just because you're not getting paid doesn't mean you're not getting valuable experience. It's not against the rules to talk about this kind of work on your CV or during your job search. Relevant experience is always, always, always valid.

Your new CV structure

YOUR NAME

+44 (0) XXXXXXX · hello@gmail.com ·
Twitter: @alexashoen · Portfolio: www.myportfolio.com

SKILLS & QUALIFICATIONS

Skill (X years)   Skill (X years)
Skill (X years)   Skill (X years)
Skill (X years)   Skill (X years)
Skill (X years)   Skill (X years)

NICE TO MEET YOU, EMPLOYER!

Hi, I'm Alexa. I'm a copywriter, creative director, and digital marketing specialist. I work across a lot of different mediums, but it always comes back to the same thing: I'm obsessed with clarity, creativity, the user journey, and comms as a retention tool.

EXPERIENCE

Company Name · Town/City, Country

Your Job Title · Month 20XX–Present
Limit yourself to 3–4 bullet points per company, with the most impressive bullet point at the top

Company Name · Town/City, Country

Your Job Title · Month 20XX–Present
Limit yourself to 3–4 bullet points per company, with the most impressive bullet point at the top

EDUCATION

University Name · Town/City, Country

Course name and result · Graduation date

The Contact section

Always remember that a CV is only *starting* its journey the moment you hit send. Your PDF is likely headed into a tracking system of some kind, somewhere, so it needs to stand on its own two feet. To illustrate: you might have emailed your application to a recruiter, but you still need to include your email address on the CV so that their colleague knows how to find you if they stumble across this document in a digital folder five weeks from now.

When I say a CV is a fluid document, I mean that *even your contact information* can change slightly depending on the types of jobs you want. Keep it on the simpler side for the more formal industries (like banking, healthcare, or insurance). For more informal or creative environments, you can and should use the Contact section strategically. Include your Instagram handle, link to your personal website, don't be afraid to show off the things that make you *you*.

My entire career, I've applied to jobs which require strong writing skills. I know that any sentence I write — on my CV, in an email, on Twitter, wherever — is a writing sample for a potential employer to judge. When it comes to how I live my life online, I am conscious of this. When it comes to my contact section, I have always included social media handles and a link to my portfolio. I'm charming and articulate online. I *want* my future co-workers to see that side of me. I *want* them to assess my work based on this additional information. The way I see it, I am just making it easy for them to find what they will probably go creeping for on their own anyway.

Make these decisions for yourself on a job-by-job basis. You have to gauge the formality level of the company, and adapt each CV specifically for that situation. Perhaps that sounds like overkill when we haven't even got past the Contact section yet. The trick is to remember throughout this entire process that there are no set-in-stone rules.

TIP

When was the last time you got any mail from a potential employer, unless it was an official contract you were about to sign because you got the job? And in that case, they're going to email you to confirm your mailing address anyway, because this is not 1974. Don't worry about putting your physical address on your CV just because you heard you were supposed to, especially if you are planning to relocate. Save the space for something that matters.

Skills & Qualifications

I love this section, and I put it right at the top of any CV I touch. Why? This is your TL;DR executive summary moment. Effectively, you're BuzzFeed-ifying your CV.

You should be able to read your own CV with the same ease that you can read an internet listicle on *The 14 Reasons Why Friends Will Always Be the Greatest Sitcom of All Time*. You've likely heard the same crazy fact I have: that recruiters spend something like eight seconds on your application before making a decision. Your CV needs to be skimmable. Give hiring managers the hard facts they're looking for right off the bat, in the most easy-to-digest way possible. With the skills section, you get the chance to highlight 8–12 of your most tangible skills immediately. You get to spell out exactly what you can offer, instead of asking recruiters to read between the lines and figure out whether any of your past experience is helpful for them.

SKILLS & QUALIFICATIONS

Social media content and scheduling (2.5 years)

Copy for physical packaging (2.5 years)

Online community management (2.5 years)

Public relations & press writing (5 years)

Copy/concepting for advertising (5 years)

SEO-driven content creation (1.5 years)

Copywriting for mobile/in-app (1.5 years)

Startup savvy: Berlin, San Fran (2.5 years)

Spanish B2 proficiency (5+ years)

Learning A2 German (an ongoing mission)

If you're an expert in Adobe Photoshop or InDesign, for example, you would put that here if it's relevant to the job you're applying for. A long time ago, it was traditional to put your skills at the bottom of your CV, where you would half-heartedly mention that you knew both Apple and PC operating systems and felt comfortable using Microsoft Excel. We've moved so far past that. If you work on a computer day-to-day, you obviously know how to use a computer and create a Word doc.

Highlight the things you know. List the technical programs you're familiar with (like writing code in C++ or sending out newsletters with MailChimp), as well as the less tangible offline skills (facilitating 30-person workshops or your experience teaching children with disabilities). You could also use this opportunity to showcase leadership stuff (like how you're the on-site lead for a four-person team in a shop).

Yes, you'll reiterate this stuff further down the page and give more context. At the end of the day, people just want to know whether or not you've got the skills to do the job you say you want. Try to keep the skills short and sweet, four to five words apiece. *Skimmable.*

> **TIP**
> This section can be flexible, too. Reorder the skills as needed. Put the most relevant skills for that particular position right at the top.

It's Nice To Meet You (optional)

Good/bad news: in my experience, up to 50% of recruiters don't read, or even open, your cover letter. I know, it's annoying. You'll probably still have to write one anyway for a ton of positions for the next decade while employers figure their stuff out. But instead of wasting time getting frustrated, look for opportunities to work around the quirks of the system.

If your CV needs to operate as a stand-alone opportunity to impress whoever is reading it, this Nice To Meet You section acts as a way to sneakily add a micro-sized cover letter, to set the narrative for everything else on the page. And it might just be the only shot you get.

> **WARNING**
> This is *not the same* as those silly Objective sections where you're supposed to write that you're looking for a job that can utilise your unique skillset. That often ends up being wasted space.

The goal of this lightweight 'elevator pitch' section is simply to make your CV come to life and get noticed — as if you yourself could magically reach through the computer screen, say hello, make a little polite small talk, shake some hands. Look, recruiters will always notice somebody with good manners. People instinctively want to hire the people they'd be willing to get stuck in traffic with — for better or worse. Whenever you get stressed out during this process, close your eyes and remember (again) that you're just trying to introduce yourself to a human being. Your introduction should be two to three lines long.

Hello, Facebook London!

I'm Alexa, and I'm a senior UX copywriter/communication designer/content strategist/whatever we're calling 'us' this week. I specialise in collaborating with designers at B2C companies like Zalando, Rocket Internet, and GetYourGuide.

Let's take this real example from my past and break it down. I'll highlight how I'm approaching this section, and why it's different to the dumb old-fashioned objective thing.

Hello, Facebook London!

Go ahead and shamelessly add their name right in the header. Nice to meet you, Facebook. Nice to meet you, United Nations. Nice to meet you, Hearst. The recruiter will do a double take, I guarantee it. You know how people say the sound of your own name is the most beautiful sound in the world? This is the professional equivalent of that. If all you get is those eight seconds, you need to use every minor attention-to-detail trick you can in order to hook someone's attention. Simple and stupid as it may seem, popping the employer's name into the header will immediately make a recruiter stop and think: Wow, nice touch. They really meant to send this CV to us. We're not just another copy-and-paste job, they actually know they're applying to work for our team.

You are going to customise your CV for every employer (yes, you are), so you might as well spend the extra few minutes to do it correctly. Employers really aren't used to people going the extra mile and creating a CV specifically tailored to the right company and role. It's these last-mile touches that will get you noticed.

I'm Alexa

If you're looking at this elevator pitch and thinking, *I have no idea what I'm going to write here*, just start by introducing yourself the same way you would in person or on the phone. Be friendly, be yourself, be honest, be as natural as you can be. Here's what a forgettable introduction would look like:

> Junior customer service manager seeking opportunity to use my customer service management skills to improve customer satisfaction.

That's a missed opportunity. Somebody who wants to work in customer service should be warm, friendly, and passionate about making people happy. The goal is to show people who you are, not just tell them.

> I'm Thomas: a junior customer service manager in the Cambridge area. I feel accomplished when I see happy customer emails in my inbox, and I know how important consistent service is to a growing company like [Company Name].

If you're worried about not having enough specialist knowledge or experience, try using this section to tell people who you are and how hard you're willing to work. Take your shot. For example:

> I'm Natalia: your next junior sales associate. I have a demonstrated track record of succeeding in customer-facing positions and there's nobody who will work harder to make sure that [Company Name] clients feel welcome and valued.

Experience

To talk about experience, we must first talk about the fictional CV police we have all hired to keep watch inside our own heads.

If you're anything like me, you want to be an honest person. There's a real difference, however, between honesty and selling yourself short — and we often confuse the two when we sit down to explain our professional experience in bullet point form. We instinctively and subconsciously decide that we'd rather undersell ourselves *just in case* someone calls us out for lying. Get caught lying and you'll never get the job, right?

When I was working at Facebook, a friend on the inside casually asked me if I was considering applying for a management position she thought I might want. 'Have you managed before?' she asked me.

'Not officially, no,' I mindlessly answered. 'Not in the context of a big company, anyway.'

'So you have managed. You know the answer is always yes, when someone asks.'

I wasn't taking my own advice: that relevant experience doesn't always come from official, real, salaried jobs. When I was running my own consulting practice, a client put me in charge of hiring and managing a team of 20 freelance writers for a massive eight-month-long project. Another client had me hire and mentor a team of nine interns one summer. I acted as interim CMO of a fashion company in the lead-up to Berlin Fashion Week and hired a team of four. The year after I started #ENTRYLEVELBOSS, I wrote up a job description for a marketing assistant who I then proceeded to source, interview, hire, train, and manage. What I hadn't done: been a salaried employee who was in charge of another salaried employee.

Nope, no management experience. Not here. Not me.

There is no CV police that knows your financial history, or how your past employer's departments and hierarchies were organised, and they certainly don't know where you live. Skills don't always come explicitly from the workload that was originally assigned to you, you know? If you did the work of five people or took on more responsibility than was originally planned, please talk about it. The CV police is not going to stomp into your next interview, sirens wailing, screaming about how you shouldn't be allowed to claim that you know a certain skill because of ... some reason you made up in your own head that validates why that experience shouldn't count.

Aagya, now based in Brooklyn, talked to me about the importance of being thoughtful and creative when it comes to demonstrating your experience:

> After deciding not to pursue an MD/PhD, I wanted to go into the business side of healthcare. I thought that no one would hire me and that I would have to go to grad school, so I took the GMAT and got into a Master's programme. But, in the meantime, I also worked REALLY HARD on my CV. I used my experience as part of class council and student government to talk about leading teams and executing programs. I landed myself numerous interviews and ultimately turned down the Master's place because I had already accepted a job in commercial strategy and operations at a top-tier consulting firm.

All my best copywriting secrets

Why is it that Very Professional CVs insist on sucking all joy out of the written word? If you've always thought your CV's grammar sounded a little funny — like you were forcing yourself to write as the old-fashioned-and-yet-also-somehow-robotic version of yourself —you're going to appreciate how simple I'm going to make this for you.

When you try to use the fancy, formal, ridiculously corporate tone that you're 'supposed' to use on CVs, you're actually making it a lot harder for recruiters and hiring managers to understand what you've accomplished. If you think something on your CV reads awkwardly, *it probably does*. If you think something on your CV is hard to understand, *it probably is*. It's not like there's some secret class of people out there who only speak Corporate English. Recruiters and employers are just people, and they're only taking those eight seconds to skim through your CV. You can't afford to have them spend half that time trying to decode your nonsensical sentences.

In no particular order, here are all the copywriting rules you need to follow. Your goal is to use language that is plain, simple, and readable. If you can't understand it, nobody else can either.

Start each experience bullet point with an action verb:

- I run
- I organise
- I create

If you already left that job, switch to past tense:

- I ran
- I organised
- I created

After the action verb (I run) part, finish each bullet point with the reason *why* you do what you do. The construction of the sentence will look like this:

- I run _____ so that _____
- I organise _____ to help _____

Example: *I run* a company called #ENTRYLEVELBOSS *to help* job seekers get hired faster with less overwhelm.

(Aside from creating an easy-to-read sentence, you are signalling to the recruiter that you know your bigger purpose. You not only know how to complete a task, but you understand *why* that task is useful to the business or organisation. This positions you as more senior and strategic.)

Use numbers whenever possible, to support your case:

- Hours you saved
- Customers you served
- Clients you helped
- Number of team members you worked with
- Money you made for the business, or funds you raised

(There are pretty much only two reasons you're going to get hired: you can either help save somebody some time, or help make somebody some money. The easiest way to prove it is to give cold, hard facts as often as possible in the form of numbers and figures.)

> **Example:** I created a simple-to-use spreadsheet system to better organise our data, saving senior management an estimated **5–7 hours** per month.
> **Example:** I developed a **year-long** marketing strategy to raise awareness about the homeless shelter near our university that reached over **70,000 students and staff**.
> **Example:** I responded to **30–40 customer service emails daily**, by personally explaining the product or directing the customer to the right contact.

(Numbers help recruiters quickly decipher the scale of your work. 'A marketing strategy about homelessness' doesn't paint a specific enough picture. They have no additional context for your projects outside of what you tell them. Don't let people assume you only put up one flyer about a bake sale, when you could give them the numbers they need to understand your work properly.)

Aim for order of importance instead of quantity:

- Put the shiniest achievement in the first bullet point, to catch people's eye.
- Don't write down five bullet points when you only need three to paint the picture.
- Give people the information they need and no more. They need the most specific information you can offer them, written in the smallest number of words.

Education
Finally, the Education section, down at the bottom. Universities and schools often tell you to list your educational achievements right up at the top — which is great advice if you're literally still in education. But then what? If it's been a few years and you've been holding off on doing so, it's time to rip off the plaster and put your educational achievements firmly below your work experience section.

I know it can be tempting to cling to your degrees and qualifications, to try and use them as a shield. 'But I have a degree,' you might feel the need to whimper. 'Yes, I graduated four years ago, but I got a first!'

I think you already know what I'm going to say about this after the chat we had in Step 2. If you are a graduate, at some point soon you need to stop telling people you went to university. The further away your graduation date sinks into the sands of time, the less and less relevant that achievement becomes. Clinging to your degree actually works in the opposite way that you'd like it to — as a red flag instead of a gold star. Why is this degree you finished four years ago still the most important thing in your professional background? You need to move on. Continue achieving rather than continue wishing your diploma could act as a makeshift life raft. It will not hold you.

Bonus: CV and cover letter formatting

Always remember that the documents you're submitting are at the beginning of a beautiful journey. At smaller companies, but sometimes even at big ones, too, this 'journey' is not as elegant as you might think. Recruiters might just be throwing every CV they get in a giant Dropbox folder, for example. If you don't title your CV clearly, you're making this process more difficult for someone else — because you just sent them a doc titled *Coverletter.pdf* which can't be distinguished from any of the other docs they received today from the other 25 candidates.

A more helpful solution:

FirstNameLastName_WhatThisDocIs_CompanyName_ JobTitle_DateYouApplied.pdf

See, it looks just like this:

AlexaShoen_CV_GringottsBank_Analyst_March2019.pdf
AlexaShoen_CoverLetter_GringottsBank_Analyst_ March2019.pdf

You will be making someone else's job easier, showing off how organised you are, and — bonus Jedi mind trick — associating your name with that position simply based on the way you titled your attachment. Neat.

PS: Always send your attachments as PDFs instead of Word documents. The fonts and formatting can get screwed up in doc files, but PDFs always look the same no matter what.

Step 3 task list

1. **Start with your Experience section.** Use my copywriting tips to deconstruct the last-known version of your CV, and re-architect it with this simplified structure.
2. **Find a friend you trust, and ask them for their feedback.** Do they understand it? Can they recite back to you what they think you did in that job? Make tweaks accordingly.
3. **Put that polished Experience section into context.** Reformat your whole CV using the #ENTRYLEVELBOSS structure.

Step 4: How to write the perfect cover letter

Since we're among friends here, we can call spade a spade. I'll even go first:

Cover letters are silly. They are old-fashioned and stupid, and they don't make any sense. You always sound like you're begging for the job. You also somehow sound like you would literally rather set yourself on fire than get the job. How is it possible to sound this arrogant and also like you have no confidence at exactly the same time? Why must we be forced to cobble together this awkwardly regurgitated poetry-slam performance-art piece? Oh, and a 2017 #ENTRYLEVELBOSS survey found that nearly half of hiring managers admit to not even reading them. This is torture and it's pointless and it's stupid and we hate them.

Go ahead, let it out, release a primal scream or something.

You good? Cool, because you still have to write one.

The good, the bad, the ugly

I used to think that if I could craft the most perfect cover letter on the planet, I would be set for life. I would convince companies to fall at my feet, charmed by my desire to #hustle and #learn thanks to this #exciting #opportunity. Yes, yes, I was one cover letter away from becoming the most hireable woman in the world. Oddly, this turned out not to be the case. As we covered in Part 1, the digitisation of the hiring process (see page 25) left us with some peculiar artefacts of the past — and cover letters are always my favourite example whenever I get the chance to point out glitches in the Matrix.

Think about the phrase for a minute: *cover letter*. Similar to *rewind* or *phone call*, the words are just haphazard leftovers from the past. From a simpler time, when an employer would put a classifieds ad in the local newspaper and receive CVs in the physical mail. The cover letter would have literally been sitting right on top, *covering* the CV. Physically covering it. Because they were, you know, printed on real sheets of paper. In that day and age — which, by the way, I never lived through and yet I, too, was told to put an employer's postal address at the top of the page — a cover letter was your one big moment. It was your only chance.

Imagine the employment world before LinkedIn, Facebook, Twitter, or Google searches. There was no one-click way for a potential employer to stalk you or gain context about you beyond what you yourself had provided. You just read about that job posting in the paper, sent in an application, and waited for a reply — probably by owl or something. The only thing anyone would ever know about you were those words written right there on the page (which really explains the entire plotline of Leonardo di Caprio and Tom Hanks' 2002 masterpiece, *Catch Me If You Can*, if you think about it).

Dear Sir,

I hope this physical piece of paper finds you in good health. I am writing to enquire about the recent advertisement for the role of experienced backgammon player, which I saw listed in the *Old-Fashioned Newspaper* on the 3rd of February, 1923. I have ten years of experience playing the game of backgammon and have won 87 of my last 144 matches. If you would be so kind as to write me back promptly, I would take the train to the big city in one fortnight's time so that I might discuss the specifications of this role with you in person.

In 2017, the #ENTRYLEVELBOSS team surveyed 200 hiring managers and recruiters across the United States and United Kingdom about how they filter candidates and make final decisions about who gets the job. One of our questions was, 'What are you looking for in a cover letter that you can't find in a CV?' More than 70% of survey responses referenced *personalisation* and *a candidate's motivation for joining the company*.

Not every role needs a great writer, and hiring managers understand that. They aren't looking for anything magical, they just want context about who you are and why you've decided to apply for the job. Why do you want to work for this team? Why? It's not an exam, it's just an honest question that you should be able to answer. Why spend all your waking hours working on *this* project, selling *this* kind of product, with *these* people?

Cover letters are a passionate topic for both hiring managers and job seekers alike — everyone's got something to say. During the many conversations I had while writing this book, two specific comments stuck with me.

The first is this beautiful rant from Danae, an American engineer turned chief marketing officer based in Edinburgh. I think she speaks on behalf of hiring managers everywhere with her ten pieces of sage wisdom for job applicants. In her own words:

For me, it's ALL about the cover letter. It's my secret weapon for hiring amazing people. Cover letters give me context. I view it as your number one competitive advantage in a job application. Here are my tips:

1. **Write a cover letter!** I don't think I have ever hired anyone who didn't have a fantastic cover letter. Without it, your CV is a cold, faceless document on a heap of identical, faceless documents. A cover letter is my first impression. Before I do anything else, I'm getting to know you by what you say. Say something.

2. **Give me context.** A fantastic cover letter gives me context for what I'm about to see in your CV. It's where you can add colour to the lifeless bullet points. This is where you can say things like 'I've never worked in your industry but my experience in X has a lot of similarities' or 'My internship was only three months long but I completed three successful projects in that time' or something like that.

3. **Tell me why you applied for this specific job.** Is it because you love the industry? Love the company's mission? Read a great article about us and feel like you could contribute because of your X experience? Tell me.

4. **Tell me a story.** Human beings love stories. Did you just come back from a gap year and realise that you really need to work in industry X because of Y? Tell that story!

5. **Make it scannable.** I remember one fantastic cover letter where the applicant (who was pretty much entry-level) used emoji to punctuate the four key strengths she brought to that job. Each one was its own short, scannable paragraph and gave me a lot of context about her and her work really quickly. I hired her. Bullet points

and short sentences are your friend. Assume I'm going to read 200 of these applications.

6. **Remember my needs.** You need a job, but I need someone who can do the job — so please don't tell me that you're applying to expand your skillset in Y or because you just love industry Z without also telling me what's in it for me. I'm not running a charity, I need to know what you're going to bring to the table.

7. **Don't be too formal.** I am not a Sir. Please don't call me Ma'am. This is your opportunity to be human, to be more relaxed. It's okay to simply say, 'I would love to work here because ...'

8. **Don't go zany/ironic.** When you're new to the professional world it's hard to know where the line is, but I'd suggest avoiding memes, jokey sarcasm, or anything 'edgy'. I once had someone jokingly write about sex toys during a writing exercise. I did not hire that person.

9. **Don't be needy.** Please don't say, 'I can work any hours, I can come in at weekends, I really just need this job.' It puts the hiring manager in a really difficult position (because they know how desperate you are) and can disadvantage you.

10. **Play back my words.** If I say I'm looking for someone with X experience and Y skills, use those words to explain yourself. Say, 'My experience in Z shows how I have mastered Y skillset.' To start your cover letter, pull out the top requirements and use that as a rough outline to structure your thoughts. Prove to me point by point that I'd be crazy not to progress you.

On the job seeker side, I read dozens of compelling cover letters; I've heard a bunch of success stories, and listened to many tales of cover letters gone wrong. No one, however, put it as beautifully as Julianne from California. Three separate times to date, Julianne has been able to explain her way into roles thanks, in no small part, to three killer cover letters. In her own words:

My first job out of university was teaching hands-on environmental science to children for a non-profit programme. Unlike everyone else in the same position, I had no background in education or environmental science. Instead, I had degrees in African History and Physical Anthropology. But I wrote a thoughtfully constructed cover letter highlighting personal attributes that I believed were relevant to the position: my public speaking and communication abilities, my passion for the environment, and my interest in and understanding of biology (shout out to physical anthro!). I was invited to interview for the position and was offered the job the next day.

I was equally 'unqualified' for my second job: working as a support counsellor for at-risk foster teenage girls. The position called for experience in social work, of which I had none. Again, I wrote a thoughtful cover letter emphasising my work with kids (from the previous job) as well as my empathy and compassion. I was invited to interview and again offered the job.

My third job had nothing to do with education, social work, African history, or anthropology. It was a project manager position at a marketing agency. Once again, I pulled relevant details from my academic and professional background and wove them together into a compelling cover letter that led to an interview. After several (probably annoying) follow-up emails, I was offered the position. I have worked in marketing ever since.

Of course, my killer cover letters alone weren't what got me these jobs. But my interview skills and persistence wouldn't have counted for anything if my cover letters hadn't got me in the door.

I found employment in education, social work, and marketing, all with two seemingly totally unrelated degrees. But the thing is, I don't actually think my degrees were totally unrelated. Both History and Anthropology require excellent communication skills. Both also centre on a deep understanding of humans. And it turns out communication and understanding people are integral to education, social work, and marketing.

For example, when I graduated, all I had on my CV under work history was seven years working at surfing shops. I also decided to include the one summer in high school when I gave surfing lessons to kids. So when I described my work history on my CV for the environmental education position I made sure to emphasise my (very informal) teaching experience: that as a supervisor I'd trained X number of sales associates and X number of new supervisors, and as a surf instructor I'd taught kids how to surf. It wasn't much compared to other applicants who had been teaching assistants in schools for years, but it was enough to show that I was able to teach someone something. I figured it was better than nothing. And, hey, combined with a killer cover letter, it worked!

Every job since then, I have done the same thing. When I applied for the support counsellor position and all I had on my CV were surfing shops and environmental education, I focused on the fact that 25% of the students I taught were considered 'at-risk'. Sure, it was only a quarter of the students I worked with, but it would have been foolish of me to leave 'at-risk' off of my CV when applying for a position working with 'at-risk' foster teenage girls.

When I applied for the project manager position, I knew that my experience selling surfboards, teaching kids about birds, and working with troubled foster youth wouldn't be wildly compelling. I focused on other aspects of those jobs instead. When I described my time working in surfing shops, I emphasised the fact that I was promoted from sales associate to supervisor in just two months to underscore my strong work ethic and ability to learn quickly. When I described my time teaching, I highlighted how I was the only one in my cohort to be invited to become a lead instructor and how I was asked to write articles for their monthly newsletter once they realised this woman can write. And when I described my work with the foster girls, I focused on logistics: tracking stipend budgets for each of my clients, organising home visits with a wide cast of characters (social workers, lawyers, foster parents, biological parents, IEP mentors, etc.), and developing and implementing individualised incentive plans.

I've never cared much about titles because focusing too much on titles can be very limiting. Just because I had never been a teacher didn't mean I had never taught someone. Just because I had never been a support counsellor didn't mean I couldn't support someone. And just because I had never been a project manager didn't mean I couldn't manage a project.

Long story short: you might be better equipped for a new field than you realise, you just need to get creative and find a way to make what you've got work for you.

The templates

I'm going to walk you through two different cover letters formats. Both of these formats are based word for word on real cover letters from my past that have successfully got me an interview at some point in my life. That doesn't mean, in the slightest, that these are the only two right answers — far from it. Every company will have its own preferences. Every cover letter you write will be different. Every situation will be unique. It will be entirely up to you to tell your story, but I can help you figure out where to start.

Cover Letter 1

Hi [Company Name],

I'm Alexa: a copywriter who works with product teams. I've collaborated with UX designers and engineers at consumer-facing tech companies like [Client/Past Employer 1], [Client/Past Employer 2], and [Client/Past Employer 3] — and I'm hoping that [Company Name] is up next.

A San Diego native, I've spent the last three years working alongside the best and brightest in Berlin tech. I'll be moving to London in January 2017 thanks to TechCity UK's Exceptional Talent Visa Scheme.

I've been watching [Company Name] from afar for the last few years and I really dig your style. You're leading the market in [thing you have observed the company is good at]. I can see the team's dedication to [something even more specific]. Your [specific detail about their product, their marketing, their business model] is a clear testament to [a value that you also value]. I love the way you [cite a specific example you've noticed, something to demonstrate that you are already thinking critically about where you could be helpful]. I worked on [briefly mention a project that shows you know how to handle this kind of thing] for six months last year.

I'm excited about the opportunity to join your team as a [role], because I know that I could help you continue to [specific task/project/thing you'd like to help the company with]. I'm fascinated by figuring out how to [cite a problem you see company facing], and I know that my experience in [skill the position requires] and [other skill the position requires] could help you solve that problem. Looking forward to chatting more soon.

Warmly,

Alexa

PS: [Brief observation about being a customer of the company ('I love that new product!') or comment about a recent press piece ('Congrats on the new partnership with So-and-So!')]

Casual language: informal vs. unprofessional

The first thing you'll notice in the above cover letter is that the tone is friendly, casual, and warm.

While there are certain industries (finance and law come to mind) where a formal tone is still appreciated, the vast majority of work environments have begun to move on. The formal tone doesn't feel natural when you try to write that way — and I promise that it doesn't feel natural to the ear of the 35-year-old recruiter who's filtering through applications on the other side of the screen, either. Write down 'To Whom It May Concern' on a piece of paper and burn it over a candle tonight, if you feel like it.

You and I both know all the clichés about millennials and Generation Z: we're entitled, we're arrogant, we don't want to work hard, we're soft, we can't take feedback. Look, there's a huge difference between being friendly and being edgy — and it could lose you the job if you get it wrong. A cover letter, for example, is probably not the right place for shock factor. It is certainly not the right place to call your new co-worker, a person whom you likely haven't met before, a pet name like 'babe' or 'love'.

Think of your new professional voice as a slow shift from 1970s business attire into 2020s business attire. You've invented an updated, modern version of a timeless classic. You *are* young, fresh, sharp talent — and you get to sound like it. The sign-off I use ('Warmly') is a good example of striking the right balance in tone. (I also like 'Cheers' and 'Thanks' and 'Speak soon', to give you a couple of other ideas!) It's friendly, modern, professional, confident, but still professional-sounding. Not too sassy, not too stuffy, just right.

First, introduce yourself

Cover Letter 1 offers a great example of the most precious, most important, most helpful, most job-getting copywriting tip I can ever give you. It's something you should do on cover letters and on

LinkedIn and in networking emails alike: introduce yourself.

Imagine how a cover letter would sound if it was read out loud in real life. Without an introduction, you quickly become some stranger with a name tag who's wandering up to people on the streets and asking for a job. Bizarre. Rude, even. Because how do all conversations start? With introductions. With a name. Introductions offer you a way to start building rapport with your future colleagues immediately, simply by translating basic offline manners onto the page.

People like classifying each other. I haven't lived in San Diego since I was 18 years old. Regardless, the words 'originally from San Diego' tumble out of my own mouth multiple times a week. It's human instinct to want to know where somebody's from, where they live now, and why they're approaching you. Think back to all those scenes in *Game of Thrones* in which Daenerys announces her own presence — with authority and eye contact — by saying that she's 'of the House Targaryen, First of Her Name, the Unburnt, Queen of the Andals and the First Men, Khaleesi of the Great Grass Sea, Breaker of Chains, and Mother of Dragons'. By giving a quick synopsis of her home town and CV, she provides her new allies and enemies with enough context to do the instinctive human work of assessing danger, skill, trustworthiness, and potential. This is your opening paragraph — people need context before they can care about anything else you're going to say.

Harvard social psychologist Amy Cuddy explains the two dimensions people intuitively scan for during the first impression moment:

When we form a first impression of another person it's not a single impression — we're really forming two. We're judging how warm and trustworthy the person is, and that's by trying to answer the question, 'What are this person's intentions towards me?' And we're also asking ourselves, 'How strong and competent is this person?' That's really about whether or not they're capable of enacting their intentions. Research shows that these two trait dimensions account for 80 to 90 percent of an overall first impression, and that holds true across cultures.

Leverage human instinct and introduce yourself.

Start with a quick recap, Daenerys-style, that tells your future employer who you are and what you're about. This is the opposite of the advice I learned from my own university career advisors. This old-school approach might look familiar to you ...

1. ~~Talk about your excitement for the company.~~
2. ~~Talk about your excitement for the position being offered.~~
3. ~~Mention your skills ('With my experience in XYZ, I believe I am a good candidate for ...').~~

Throw it out. Don't do this. It's weird and formal and wrong. Your first and second paragraph should provide an answer to *Who are you and why are you in my inbox?*

Next, turn your attention to them

In Cover Letter 1, I use paragraphs three and four to subtly demonstrate that I've done my homework. I talk about how I've been watching this company grow. I tell them about a pattern I've noticed in their marketing. I quickly try to highlight what I've seen to be true from an outsider's perspective.

If paragraph three is all I've-noticed-you-and-think-you're-cute flirtation, then paragraph four is your chance to step up to the plate and announce that you're here to help. Notice my second sentence: 'I'm fascinated by figuring out how to ____, and I know my experience in ____ and _____ could help you solve that problem' I'm already hinting at ideas for where I think I could provide value, and I don't even have the job yet.

Never forget how valuable an outside perspective is to any organisation, throughout the entire job search process. Leverage your outsider perspective whenever possible. The 'can't see the forest for the trees' phenomenon is a dangerous but common poison for businesses. Experienced candidates (for senior or executive level roles) will often be asked to critique a company's performance on something *without* context so that the company can discover and correct problematic assumptions that are being made internally.

The 'PS' section

This is an opportunity to infuse your application with one extra personalised moment in order to start building that relationship with (fingers crossed) your future co-worker. Use the space to inject a just-between-us quip that will snap the reader back to attention so that they're inspired to go back and read from the beginning if they haven't already.

> **Example:** I bought the new Chelsea boots that you guys have been hyping on Instagram and am now obsessed. Should have bought two pairs.

Including a 'PS' section is huge strategic tool in email marketing. People read so much content on their phones all day long that they're prone to want to skim everything. Good marketers know that, and they plan for it. Because of where the PS is located on the page, at the bottom, you will catch the people who have only been skimming — and, if nothing else, you will reaffirm that you have gone the extra mile in order to personalise.

The basic structure to follow

First, it's about you ...

Paragraph 1: Introduce yourself and what you do.

Paragraph 2: Provide more context about yourself or your skillset.

Then, it's about them ...

Paragraph 3: Talk, as specifically as possible, about why you want to join this company.

Paragraph 4: Talk, as specifically as possible, about how you plan on helping them achieve their goals.

Cover Letter 2

I hate cover letters as much as journalists hate pitches, so I'm going to give you four good reasons you should hire me in listicle format:

1. You really won't find a better people connector. I'm a winning conversationalist in everything from accelerators to music tech to Las Vegas dive bars.
2. I know events have a lot of moving parts — and guests shouldn't feel that. I'm calm and user-friendly, no matter what's happening behind the Authorised Personnel door.
3. I live in Berlin, which is a good thing for you. You need someone who is fluent in multiple tech scenes and multiple cultures. I can sympathise with SF jetlag, talk a bit of Londoner, and root for continental startups all in one conversation.
4. My favourite motto is this: If you're only networking when you want something, you're doing it wrong.

In all seriousness, I think I'd be a great asset to the media team. Please do get in touch so that we can chat a bit more about what you're looking for in a candidate, and how I might be able to help.
Cheers,
Alexa

As you can clearly see, Cover Letter 2 is far too specific to me and my life to be followed line by line. Please don't do that, it would be super weird of you.

I offer it up as a reminder that you can break any and all rules regarding what you think a job application 'should' look like. A reminder that magic can happen and doors can open when you break the rules in a way that strikes the right chord with the right hiring manager. Magic can happen when you find your people and signal that you, too, are one of them.

This cover letter — which is, word for word, exactly what I sent in with an application — would read as arrogant and obnoxious to the wrong audience. The reason I knew I could pull off this kind of tone had little to do with the role and much more to do with the company itself. They had a reputation for bravado. I knew that approaching them with a high-powered alpha vibe would work. Lo and behold, I sent in an application (out of the blue, without having any connections whatsoever with any employees) and got an invitation to interview within a couple of weeks.

One part comedy, one part respect

If the sassiness of Cover Letter 2 appeals to you, please note the crucial tone change in the last paragraph. I leave things on a more professional, more respectful note — poking fun at my own bravado. I've successfully illustrated that I can be charming and cutting edge, but at the end of the day, I know this is a business situation and not a theatre production.

In defence of the listicle format

Beloved by the internet, the listicle is basically a numbered list of paragraphs. The listicle is a way to structure an argument. This is a blade to wield carefully in a professional context. It can read as over-done or cheesy. The underlying concept of skimmability remains crucial to a successful job application, though. The recruiter on the other side of the screen is reading the same *19 Ways To Tell Your Dog You Love Her This Valentine's Day* articles that you are, meaning that their brain will be attuned to digesting content in this style.

As British journalist Steven Poole puts it:

> The listicle is seductive because it promises upfront to condense any subject into a manageable number of discrete facts or at least factoids. When you embark on reading an ordinary article, you have no way of knowing how many things it will tell you. Maybe 15, maybe two. Frustrating. Plus, if you're reading online and it's more than a single screen long, you can't be sure when it's going to end. A listicle keeps helpfully informing you how much of it there is left.

While the tone I use in Cover Letter 2 might be entirely too obnoxious for either you or your potential employer, there are ways to soften the edges and leverage the bullet point style to get your point across. People like having their expectations managed. Bullet points (or listicles) give you a straightforward way to lay out your key selling points in the cleanest way possible.

A more subtle way to leverage the listicle format

A sentence to introduce yourself and what you do.

List 1: Here are three reasons why I'm the right person for the job:

- Bullet point 1
- Bullet point 2
- Bullet point 3

List 2: Here are three things I'd be excited to tackle in this position, based on what I know so far about the company:

- Bullet point 1
- Bullet point 2
- Bullet point 3

A sentence to say you're excited about the role and want to speak more about it soon.

BONUS: LENGTH AND PARAGRAPH BREAKS

Whether I am using the listicle format or not, notice that I'm hitting return after every couple of sentences, sometimes even after one sentence. I'm doing this so that the entire cover letter (or cover email, in some cases!) is easier to skim *and* easier to read on a mobile phone.

The vast majority of email clients (like Gmail) and job application software programs are built using something called 'responsive design'. When a website is responsive, any written content expands or contracts to fit the size of the screen: laptop, tablet, mobile phone, etc. A paragraph that looks short and sweet on your laptop will take up the whole screen on your hiring manager's phone screen. Yes, someone might be looking at your application while commuting into the office.

Putting in a few extra paragraph breaks gives your words some breathing room. Your cover letter immediately seems more modern, friendly, and personable — no matter what size the screen is.

And that's all there is to it. Cover letters and first dates have a lot in common. Your goal is to be flirty and interesting and intriguing enough that they will want to call you. You don't need to explain everything in this single document, just like how you wouldn't try to tell a date your entire life story during the first meeting.

Most importantly, don't be so afraid of them. Cover letters are not the be-all and end-all, and certainly not for any positions that don't require you to be a world-class writer. It's okay to have some fun. It's okay to speak like the modern human being that you are.

Step 4 task list

1. Pick a job application you were planning to submit soon, and put one of these cover letter templates into practice. Make sure that you:
    a. Introduce yourself right off the bat.
    b. Think about the person on the other side of the screen (how would it feel if this cover letter landed in *your* inbox?).
    c. Get specific about why you're drawn to this specific employer.
    d. Get specific about what problem you want to help them solve.

Step 5: Finishing touches

I've never been fond of the term 'personal branding', even though I will admit that, kind of, yes, that's what Step 5 is about. But only kind of, and only if you really need me to admit it.

We're going to quickly cover two different topics in one fell swoop:

1. Personal branding tricks that will make you look put together both offline and online.
2. Specific guidance on maintaining your social media channels during the job search.

If you're thinking about skipping this section, because self-promotion is embarrassing and tacky and you don't want to do it, I won't be able to stop you. Many of us have been taught that, theoretically, employment decisions are all based on merit and that, theoretically, the best person will rise to the top. However, we also now know about the chaos of hiring and the 37% Rule. Still, the idea of doing anything 'extra' to set yourself apart, above and beyond stuff that's strictly related to your official professional skillset, might feel a bit like … well, cheating.

A story: I've never been a huge musical theatre person (what can I say — I always liked to freestyle on the mic too much), but

I would occasionally audition for shows when I was a kid. One summer, I auditioned for Andrew Lloyd Webber's *Jesus Christ Superstar*. I was young, maybe nine years old, but I have clear memories of the whole day because it was a pretty heavy-hitting production. I had to bring a headshot, I had to prepare a specific song from the musical in advance. There was even a choreography portion in the audition. I can't tell you which song I sang, but I vividly remember one conversation I had with a grown-up who had been to a ton of auditions.

'Wear a bright colour,' this person said to me. 'And if you get called back, wear the same bright colour again. That way, when they go away at the end of the week and talk about who they're going to cast, they can keep referring to you as *the little blonde girl in the red top* and everyone will know exactly who they're talking about.'

As much as we want to believe in the best person for the job getting the job, we also know about the haphazard imperfections of modern hiring. Being excellent is not enough. Being lucky is not enough, either, so you need to, in as many ways as possible, make sure that you are *known* to your future employer as an excellent candidate. Be clear in what you want, have a consistent message about what you can offer, put your best foot forward from the moment you make that (digital!) first impression.

Your soulmate may be sitting on the other side of the room, but if you don't notice them or understand that they are into you, you can't marry them. Feel me? (Note to self: I should probably write an *#ENTRYLEVELDATING* sequel.)

These various 'finishing touch' suggestions should help you in two distinct ways. Some of these tricks are about helping *you* feel confident when you walk into the room, because you know you have all your bases covered. Some of these tricks are about helping *them* remember you and exactly what you're about, amidst all the noise and the applicants and the distractions that they have to deal with on their end. Some will do both. Basically, these simple-to-implement tricks might ultimately make the difference between you getting noticed and you staying unemployed or underemployed.

And if that's not a strong enough pitch for you, then just know that this is the last step of your axe-sharpening journey before you're allowed to start submitting job applications again. Score.

Tricks for feeling put-together and powerful

Get yourself some professional photos

For many moons now, I've been telling people that there are two things you can still do in this modern internet world that are — for some reason — almost guaranteed to impress people: have fancy photos of yourself and become a published author. (I know, right? I get a kick out of me, too.)

You should have a great photo of yourself for LinkedIn, for your email avatar, for your social media presence, and for your personal website (if you have one).

To be clear, here's what a professional photo is not:

- You squinting in the sun in a suit that's too big for you.
- You in a blurry group photo from five years ago.
- You at the jobs fair at university.
- You at your cousin's third wedding.
- You in front of one of those weird School Picture Day backgrounds.

Good photos — and I'm talking *When our cover star arrived that morning on set, she was wearing a crisp white button-down and looked like she had a secret to tell me* full-on movie star quality — give off this air of luxury and intellect and confidence that few other things can top. And you can get one anytime you want.

Here's the psychology behind what I'm saying here: people often make an incorrect assumption that, if you have a nice professional photo of yourself, there must have been a reason for you to get one. You have a slick photo of yourself talking into a microphone? It must be because you were on stage at an important conference. You have an amazing shot of you sketching out the graphics for a new website? It must be because you were a rock star on some previous project and the employer wanted to show you off. You have a great personal portrait? It must be because you won an award and got interviewed in a magazine about it.

Chelsea, a freelance copywriter based in Sweden, saw this psychology in action when she changed her LinkedIn profile picture: 'I got contacted by an online learning platform to host a class for them out of the blue — and I'm convinced the only reason it happened is because I finally put a decent photo up.'

How to get a good photo of yourself

Pay someone. Find a local fashion photography student or someone who is just starting out in the wedding photography business. Please do not go back to your school photographer. We are going for *confident professional in a Day-In-the-Life magazine feature*, not *awkward internet meme*.

If you can't afford to hire a photographer to shoot a modern headshot right now, ask for help from whichever friend or family member has the best eye for photography. Any iPhone or Pixel photo will be high-res enough to look great on all your social media profiles. Which photo is up on your LinkedIn right now? If it's remotely close to one of the options I just made fun of, you've got to go do this. C'mon, you're on the prowl. Let's get out there and look our best, honey.

> **My only modelling tip:** Don't try to look pretty, try to look like yourself. I promise you that your photos will turn out so much better this way.

Choose a title and own it

Once you start talking to your future employers or anyone who can help you on this journey, you need to pick a job title and run fearlessly in that direction. Try to use the most common, simple, specific title you see other people using on LinkedIn or Twitter or wherever. Naming your desired position gives future employers a strong anchor for what you do, which allows them to more easily understand how to place you.

This is helpful:

> 'I am a media buying strategy professional, specialising in Google AdWords.'
> 'I want an entry-level job in regional sales for a B2B company in Sydney.'

This is NOT helpful:

> 'I'm looking to get into marketing.'
> 'I can't decide if I want to do sales or not.'
> 'I aspire to enter the social work industry.'
> 'I am looking for jobs that utilise my talents.'
> 'I want to use my communication skills to drive business outcomes.'
> 'I'm considering going into the technology industry.'

If it feels awkward to say 'I'm a business operations manager' out loud because you've never had that job before, try saying 'I'm looking for business operations manager roles' instead.

To get more comfortable with your title (new or current!), practise on strangers and the internet. I used to fumble all the time early on in my career when people asked me what I did for a living.

I felt like I was too inexperienced to be allowed to call myself a copywriter — so I forced myself into it by putting 'copywriter' as the very first word in my Twitter bio. It's silly, but it helped to see that name next to my own photo.

Get yourself a website

My first website was a nightmare. I thought I had to be able to code it myself. I was worried that I would ultimately be judged on how ugly it was, instead of being judged on the thing it was meant for: to showcase my writing and marketing work. All that fear was unfounded. A website can be really easy to make and really helpful to have. Think of it as your digital business card.

Portfolio people, listen up: If you are a writer, designer, performer, actor, dancer, videographer, marketer, editor, painter, journalist, illustrator, developer, maker, producer of anything? Having a website is a non-negotiable. People will only believe that you are what you say you are when you can clearly show them the things that you've made. If you don't have a website to showcase your portfolio yet, stop avoiding it. Your perfectionism is killing your career. It will take you one day to pull the screenshots and video links and documents and assets together. Just go do it.

All you other people: A website is a nice-to-have that might help you stand out. Keep it super simple. A nice photo, a link to your LinkedIn and other social profiles, your elevator pitch, and your email address. Whatever you want your digital business card to say about you.

You can make a website for free. For less than the cost of brunch, you can get a real domain name (like entrylevelboss. com or alexashoen.com) that makes you feel legit. With tools like Squarespace and WIX and Dribbble, building your own website is literally as easy as using Microsoft Word. I know you have heard all about this on podcast adverts, but it's actually true. No coding or design skills needed, I promise you. I do not know how to code and I make websites all the time.

Print yourself some business cards

You know what helps soothe imposter syndrome? Proof that you are who you say you are. You know how to get proof that you are who you say you are? Business cards!

The first time I decided to call myself a 'content strategist' was on a business card I printed right before moving from San Francisco to Berlin. I had already hustled to line up a boatload of meetings, meet-ups, and conferences for my first couple of weeks — and I miraculously remembered to make myself some business cards before boarding my flight. I clicked around moo.com for a while before I came up with this:

Alexa Shoen
Content Strategy / Community Management

Just 48 hours after landing, I had already passed out at least forty of these cards at my first-ever Berlin conference. And you know what? No one screamed at me for being a fraud. The opposite, actually: I got asked for my opinion on how marketing, public relations, and hiring work in the States. I was (and still am!) so grateful to myself for printing that little card.

I realise that I just said your website is your digital business card, and we *are* deep into the 21st century at this point, so physical printing might not be your thing. But if you want one, print one. The hold-it-in-your-own-hands magic of business cards might give you the boost of confidence you need to keep moving forward. Because if you say you're a Dream Job Title out loud enough times; if you write it all over your Twitter, your Instagram, your LinkedIn; *and* you have a physical rectangle that says you're that thing — well, you'd better go out and be that thing, right?

Guidelines for your social media presence

At this point, no one born in the last century can escape having some kind of digital footprint. We don't need to fight against it anymore. The internet has truly arrived, my friend, and, actually, it's been here for quite some time. One of the most helpful things you can do for your job search is to accept that your online presence *is* a part of your CV, and think about what you want that to mean for you. Any additional information that hiring managers can find online is going to be considered fair game. Don't hide from that. Leverage it.

The 20th-century professional rulebook taught us to create thick walls in between our personal life and our professional life. *Do whatever you want in private, sure, but don't talk about it too much at work. Make sure you present the safe-for-radio version of yourself at all times. Just pretend you like golf and opera. Don't have too much personality. Sit up straight. Be quiet.* If you played according to those rules, social media guidance would look like this: *Have a LinkedIn profile, keep your Instagram private, and go through your Facebook to make sure you delete all those treacherous university photos.*

I'm not remotely sold on this being your strongest online strategy. The world is changing (slowly, and it varies a ton from industry to industry, but it *is* changing). We are allowed to be whole people. We are allowed to have interests and opinions and passions. This is why I genuinely believe that having a presence on the internet will ultimately help, not hurt, your career. I believe that if you hide your personal life and your personality entirely from employers, it will backfire on you. You start by aiming for sanitised, safe, and likeable. You wind up forgettable, sterile, and unemployed. And there's a much worse outcome than that, actually — which is that you get hired. Somebody wanted this vanilla version of you. That version will have to keep showing up to work every day.

A REALLY IMPORTANT NOTE
I appreciate that what's 'appropriate' for work is a loaded topic, because of the ways in which the world prioritises heteronormative white lifestyles. Figuring out what decisions you are happy to make in how you present yourself digitally is a very personal process and will vary depending on your situation and identity, but ultimately you should make the choices that feel best for you.

Instagram and Twitter

There's no need for you to start a Twitter or an Instagram if you don't already have one (well, unless you're going into journalism or fashion or any industry that uses social media for networking). There's no need for you to spend your precious job searching hours getting more followers (well, unless you're going into social media and are using your own account to experiment and teach yourself new skills). But if you're a die-hard user of either platform or you want to join the party, I'm excited. Over the course of your job search journey, I want you to think about how to leverage these tools from the following angles:

1. **Networking.** These platforms – and any platforms like them that pop up in the future – are extremely powerful because they both operate in a way that allows random people to start conversations with each other. That kind of interaction presents us with an insanely huge networking opportunity. Gary Vaynerchuk, a well-known voice on the power of social media, often credits Twitter as the place where his career success began. He refers to the platform as 'the world's biggest cocktail party'. You should always keep your Twitter and Instagram in mind when you start thinking about your strategies for reaching out to people.

2. **Website traffic.** That little bio section is, as far as I'm concerned, another opportunity for you to put yourself and your CV out there. Add your website link. Direct traffic to your LinkedIn page, your website, your portfolio, or another social media site where you're showing off your skillset in some capacity. Think about it and get creative! Definitely don't waste the real estate.

If you want to stay private and/or social media just isn't really your thing, that's okay, but I have one super important reminder for you. Even if you're private, people can still see your profile picture and bio, so keep it classy.

Facebook

Facebook is the world's online directory for people, and plenty of employers will come looking for you on there. My recommendation? Give in to the chaos. Be smart about it. Embrace the fact that you're going to get stalked.

I keep a lot of my profile pictures set to public. If you look me up, hopefully you'll see what I would want recruiters to see: that I bring good, fun, positive energy to the table. I also keep certain posts and life announcements set to public. On my wall, you'll spot a sampling of my accomplishments and announcements from the last decade. If it shows me in a good professional light, it's out there on purpose — because, heck yeah, I want recruiters to see me in action. More personal photos stay personal, and the edgier ones stay ... off the internet.

> **TIP**
> Use Facebook's Intro section wisely. I find that it's not very noticeable to your friends, but is very noticeable to strangers who come to your profile page. Use that design feature to your advantage. For years, mine has said: *Creeping best accomplished through my weekly email: alexashoen.com/join-now/*

There's no need for you to get a Facebook profile if you don't already have one. If you're not on Facebook or you're unsearchable, that's not going to hurt your employment opportunities.

LinkedIn

When I introduce two new people by email, I hyperlink to their LinkedIn profiles. When I want to learn more about a company, I creep on their employees' LinkedIn profiles. When people want to hire me, they look at my LinkedIn profile. It is a lot easier to forward a profile URL than it is to forward a CV. In any market where LinkedIn holds the lion's share of the market, this platform cannot be ignored.

If you're not on LinkedIn by now, you need to be. If your profile is out of date, you need to fix it immediately. I know it can feel awkward to start your profile or to edit your job history. So much intimate career information, out there, for public consumption! You're exposed. *What if someone, like, actually looked at my mediocre CV? Better not.*

Dear friend, please don't waste even a single moment worrying about your CV not being good enough to be on LinkedIn. If you take anything away from this book, I want it to be this: there is no shame in looking for a job. It's time to move past your fear of being seen, of being exposed, of having someone notice that you're looking. You are making an effort to find work, to contribute your talents to an industry of your choosing, and to be an active member of the economy and of the world. You're amazing.

Whether you're completely new to the platform or you're just making updates, here are a few of my go-to LinkedIn profile suggestions:

- For the Experience section, I find that bullet points can look really stiff on LinkedIn. You do not have to phrase things the exact same way that you might phrase them on your CV if it doesn't feel right. Try to write a three-sentence summary of what you did in a role, instead of using bullet points. Look up my profile to see what I mean: linkedin.com/in/alexashoen
- For the Summary section, write a short bio right at the top. This text might look similar to the **Nice To Meet You** section from your CV (see page 93) or the **Introduction** paragraph from your cover letter (see page 115). Take inspiration from people you admire. Mess around with a few different formats or styles until it feels like you. First-person will make you stand out. Third-person might work better for more formal industries or more senior titles.

Here's a short-and-sweet professional version that I used to use:

Alexa Shoen is a content strategist who puts clarity above all else. Before joining Facebook to work on ad products in June 2017, Alexa ran her own communications practice in Berlin and pioneered the UX content strategy discipline for Zalando, Rocket Internet, GetYourGuide, and others. You can usually find her on Instagram (@alexashoen) or loitering near one of those free pianos in tube stations.

To get in touch: heyalexa@entrylevelboss.com

And here's an older, more punchy example that sold my skill-set when I was freelancing:

> I'm Alexa, a Californian copywriter based in Berlin. I like smart communications and creative marketing — which is good, because that's exactly what I'd like to do for you.

> My KPIs are typically brand awareness, user engagement, user acquisition, and — my favourite — user retention. I improve those things by writing, tweaking, and creating systems for website copy, sales pages, social media channels, social media content, newsletters, media outreach, SEO-driven blogging, video campaigns, UX clarity, events, sponsor deals, affiliate media partnerships, and more.

> Find me online at @alexashoen.

TIP
For the Summary section, paste that skills section from your CV (see page 91) directly underneath your new bio. It's a quick way to let recruiters and managers know exactly what you offer. The Summary section text is searchable, making it the perfect place for keywords. By searchable, I mean that when a recruiter types 'photoshop San Diego' into the LinkedIn search bar, your profile could come up in their search.
Even sneakier tip: Definitely utilise this skills section strategy if you're job searching while already employed. You'll make your own profile more discoverable while also remaining discreet.

LinkedIn will quickly become your favourite platform once you get the hang of it (which, don't worry, is easy to do!). It's an extremely powerful, ever-changing resource to use in your job search. To get the most up-to-date version of this advice and then some, go to **entrylevelboss.com/linkedin.**

Step 5 task list

1. **Audit your public persona.** Google yourself in Incognito mode. Check the 'logged out' version of all your social media profiles. Run a fine-toothed comb over the internet, and make the necessary edits in order to put your very best foot forward.
2. **Set up your LinkedIn profile if you don't yet have one.** If you do have one, make sure that it's up to date based on the edits you made to your CV in Step 3. Go to **entrylevelboss.com/linkedin** for more guidance.
3. **Make a prioritised to-do list of anything else you need/want to do in order to feel 100% confident before you start getting your name out there.** This list is going to vary wildly for every person, but here are a few ideas:
   a. Create (or update) your portfolio.
   b. Create (or update) your personal website.
   c. Get yourself a new photo.
   d. Print business cards.
   e. Practise your elevator pitch in the mirror.
   f. Spell-check your CV.
   g. Polish your shoes, buy a new lipstick, get a haircut, etc.

A brief interval

Let's pause — you've earned it — to grab a cup of coffee, have a snack, and check in.

The first five steps of this process are specifically designed to, above all else, reverse your panic and put you back in the driver's seat. Clarity begets success, always.

We're about to start Part 3, which means you're officially allowed to go back out in public. Applications are now fair game — though you're quickly going to learn how to leverage some insanely cool networking tricks in order to be as proactive as humanly possible and take charge of your own destiny instead of just mindlessly filling in applications.

As you come across new opportunities and meet new contacts out there in the real world, you will learn how to sharpen your axe on the go. You will continue crafting new versions of your CV and writing new versions of your cover letter. You will discover more about what you want. But I also want you to be careful out there.

Remember the job-search junk-food diet? Doesn't it *feel* like a junk-food diet now, looking back on it after everything you've just done and learned? You know how easy it is to fall back into old habits as soon as the training wheels come off, and this process is no exception. I want to take this moment to remind you that you now possess all the tools you need in order to course-correct whenever you feel like it. You can come back to your 'battle preparation' strategic steps at any time. You can retreat into your own personal job search gym, do a bicep curl, recentre your brain.

Be honest with yourself about what you need to do in order to stay on track. If you err on the side of preparation over action, push yourself in the other direction. If you err on the side of panic-sending as many applications as possible, force yourself back into the gym. What I do know is this: it takes a balanced combination of focus and bravery to get what you want in the employment market.

PAUSE

Keys, yes. Phone, yes. Wallet, yes. If I have all three, it means I can confidently leave the house for the day. We can do the same thing as we head out of the job search gym and go back into public mode. Here's what to check for:

- Your mission statement: 'I'm looking for X kind of role in Y industry in Z location'.
- A target list of the companies and organisations that you're planning to approach.
- A baseline CV that you feel good about.
- A better understanding of how to flirt in your cover letters.
- Extra collateral like your website, your social media profiles, your LinkedIn, your new photo.
- A list of concrete tactics for adding new skills to your CV (see Step 2).

What else do you need to do today (or this week) before you make your public debut? What will make you feel in control, motivated, and focused? It may help to reread the Ground Rules again (see page 38) or to print out your Target Employer List and hang it up where you can see it. Go to **entrylevelboss.com/jobsearchgym** to check out some collateral examples, get a couple more last-minute tips, and get motivated for Part 3.

Part 3

We Network, So That We Get Work

'People cannot hire me if they do not know I exist.'
Ancient #ENTRYLEVELBOSS proverb

Feeling strong? You should be, seeing as you've basically just given yourself the professional equivalent of a life-changing *Queer Eye* makeover. You are feeling your look, you know what you want, you possess a fresh mindset in your heart and mid-range beauty products in your bathroom. I mean, damn, henny, look at you serve it up. It would be tempting to stop here and go right back to the job-search junk-food diet with renewed self-confidence and a slightly sexier haircut. You might feel like you've got everything you need, and besides, you haven't submitted a job application in days. You're falling behind.

But *Queer Eye* episodes don't end at the fashion-show-in-the-redecorated-apartment part, and that's where we're at right now. The journey only comes to an end once the boys have said their goodbyes, leaving this episode's hero to enter the kitchen alone and bravely attempt to remake Antoni's avocado toast for beloved friends and family. That is the moment when the transformation — external and internal — becomes complete. (If these references elude you, then just trust me on this one. I have watched every season and also all of Jonathan Van Ness' internet ice-skating content.)

The party-after-the-makeover is when theory gets put into practice. In that moment, you get to take the new tools bestowed upon you by global pop-culture icons Karamo, Bobby, Tan, Jonathan, Antoni, and Alexa — and you go out to show the world what you can truly offer. It's the last mile. It's the only path forward. It's the only way you'll ever make it to that restaurant reopening and/or sunset proposal and/or emotional choir solo and/or new job.

Yes, it's time to network. You're ready. We're going to get you dressed in these glass slippers, pop you inside this pumpkin-coloured Uber, and get you to the ball.

Why you don't need to be scared

Before we start, I want to quell all of your fears about the 'networking' thing. In fact, you can go to **entrylevelboss.com/youcandoit** in order to watch me give you an extended version of this whole pep talk in video form.

I appreciate that the concept of networking can be nausea-inducing for many of us. The whole idea might, in fact, feel a little like cheating. (*Why should you be allowed to go and talk to people? You should politely wait at home until they get to your application. That's what's fair.*) The word itself may conjure up horrifying images in your mind that you'd rather not see come to life. (You, now somehow dressed in ill-fitting khakis and a tie, wearing a plastic badge and drinking warm white wine, awkwardly squinting up at the fluorescent ceiling lights in a mediocre hotel function room.)

I promise that I am not asking you to walk into a crowded room alone. You do not need to attend a single in-person meetup, though I'm going to give you a couple of interesting arguments as to why you should. The fitness plan that I'm prescribing doesn't actually require you to go outside at all, unless you feel like it. (Side note: how great is it that you can get your foot in the door without leaving your house? It has never been a better time to be an introvert.)

As we dive into these next pages, you'll quickly learn that I am merely asking you to play a game of 'I Spy' with the universe for a little while. Somewhere out there, right now, this second, there are strangers roaming the planet who will change the course of your career trajectory. We just need to find them. You already possess all the tools you'll ever need for this mission: a curious mind, an email account, the shadiness to send an occasional social media DM, and the ability to explain what you want from people. Easy.

If you stop reading right now, you might go back to your pile of applications feeling like you're playing ball — but you won't be. If you return to your old job search habits, you'll have never even made it onto the pitch. If you keep filling out half-hearted applications (or even good ones!) and sending them to anonymous people who have never heard of you, you are effectively standing on the sidelines pretending it's the same thing as scoring a goal at Wembley.

These networking systems I'm about to give you? They will turn water into wine, strangers into friends, and emails into employment contracts. Most importantly, you need to remember that they are *designed to be used*. If you think the networking part is optional, you'll be throwing away the hard work you just did to get this far.

If playing *I Spy* with the universe sounds way too hippie for you and scoring a goal at Wembley sounds equal parts fun and unrealistic, just stick with me a little bit longer.

The people who get us hired

Once you have a Target Employer List, networking just becomes a means to an end rather than a start-from-scratch puzzle. You know what you want and now you get to go and explicitly ask for it. These are the people you need to go out and talk to:

1. **People you already know.** Your friends, your friends' parents, your parents' friends, your former colleagues, your teachers, the people you studied with, your cousin's roommate's husband, etc.
2. **People you want to work for/with.** Any person that currently works for one of the companies on your Target Employer List.
3. **The Magical Sparks.** Any person who you'd classify as a stranger *and* who also doesn't work for one of your target companies — but might wind up getting you hired there (or, perhaps, some place cooler that you don't even know about yet).

Why these three groups?

Your network (group 1) wants to see you succeed, so this is just a simple matter of telling them what's going on and how they can help.

Your future employer (group 2) is looking for talent, but they can't hire you yet because they don't currently know you exist.

But while that all makes this game sound incredibly straightforward, destiny is rarely predictable. Enter those Magical Sparks (group 3) people. This one is the most fun game to play, because these gorgeous people are going to help you create those right-place-right-time, stroke-of-luck moments that can only really happen when you start making moves to take destiny into your own hands.

This is not merely networking. What I'm doing is teaching you how to set your own universe ablaze with possibility. Networking constantly — and I mean daily — with people from these three groups will be the single most efficient and effective thing you can do for your job search.

Your new professional networking fitness programme

	Sunday	Monday	Tuesday	Wednesday	Thursday
Person I Know	✔		✔	✔	✔
Target Employer		✔	✔		✔
Magical Spark	✔	✔		✔	

The theory of weak ties

In order to understand why I'm so all-in on the power of networking, you need to appreciate just how important weak ties are to employment ecosystems of all shapes and sizes. In 1973, an American sociology professor named Mark Granovetter published a very important and famous paper called 'The Strength of Weak Ties', which examines the impact of networking on your employment prospects. If you've ever heard anything about the concept of weak ties before, it's most likely because of this paper. Granovetter set out to demonstrate that that a person's most defining moments of progress — the new job, the introduction to a spouse, the dream home — usually depend on a tip from a stranger or almost-stranger. These strangers act as portals, catapulting us into new realities, simply because they have access to a different set of opportunities than the kind you and your close-knit friends already know about.

I appreciate that my use of the word 'portal' makes this sound like a once-in-a-lifetime occurrence, but you've probably already formed at least one weak-tie connection this month. Here's a situation we're all familiar with: let's say that Ashley and TJ are friends, and TJ and Mikey are friends. When Ashley and Mikey finally meet, they'll probably be friends, too, or at least willing to help each other out based on their mutual affection for TJ. In Granovetter's words, weak ties are easy to form 'if strong ties connect A to B and A to C' because 'both C and B, being similar to A, are probably similar to one another, increasing the likelihood of a friendship once they have met'. *Any friend of TJ's is a friend of mine!*

The theory of weak ties centres around this labour-market economics study that Granovetter conducted about how people find employment in America (in roles ranging from blue-collar to managerial professional). He polled a random sample of Boston job changers who had said they'd been hired through a contact or connection. To every one of these people, he posed the same question: how often would you say you *saw* that connection around the time when they offered to help you out? About 83% of respondents said they saw their connection 'occasionally' or 'rarely'. There's a footnote in this part of the paper where Granovetter says that whenever he asked respondents 'whether a friend had told them about their current job, they said, "Not a friend, an acquaintance."'

Acquaintances. These are our bridge-builders. Acquaintances — the almost-strangers that you barely know — are the people most likely to turn your world upside down. 'It is remarkable that people receive crucial information from individuals whose very existence they have forgotten,' Granovetter writes.

If you think this information must be out of date, you would be wrong. Just look around at all the digital platforms that try to help us leverage the magic of weak ties in our daily lives. The dating sites that show you whether or not you went to the same university. LinkedIn telling you that you have a connection in common with somebody. Instagram showing you that someone you don't yet follow is already followed by X number of people who also follow you.

Rupert, who works for a luggage company in New York, told me a particularly epic weak-tie story:

During my last job search, I did my due diligence. Every time I applied somewhere, I would go stalk all the employees I could find on social media, especially the people of colour, and see whether we had any connections in common. When I was checking out people for [the job I have now], I was looking up employees on social media and noticed that most of them were followed by this one guy who I had met in passing for 10 minutes at a bar the summer before. Literally, he had needed a seat, we made small talk while he waited for his friend, and we ended up exchanging social media details and that was it. I messaged him and was like, 'Hey, how are things going, long time no see — okay, let me cut the BS, I just applied for a job and I've noticed that you follow some people who work there. Do you work there too, or have you ever worked there? I'm trying to get a foot in the door.' And he was like, 'That's really funny, because 1. I do work there, and 2. I'm the manager of talent acquisition.' I told him which role I had applied for and he was like, 'This is crazy, I am actually looking at CVs for this position on my computer as we speak.' He checked out my CV on the spot, and when he saw how qualified I was for the job, he fast-tracked me past the phone screen and introduced me to the hiring manager. I still had to do five in-person interviews and a phone call with the CEO herself, but within a two-week period, I got that job.

The ultimate lesson, as far as you and I are concerned, is that you don't need to be worried if your best friend or brother aren't going to be the ones to hook you up with some sweet new job. They were never going to be. As Granovetter puts it, 'no strong tie is a bridge'. Your mission is to look out for the mystical acquaintances and strangers who will act as the link between the universe as you know it and the universe in which you get hired. They are the monkey bars that connect playgrounds, the snakes and ladders between narratives, the secret alleyway into the network that sits just next door to your own. Distant acquaintances, friends of friends, people you vaguely have something in common with: these are the people that change your life.

Make it stupid-easy for people to help you

Even when you know somebody, it is never good enough to just get in front of someone's face and say, 'I am sending you my CV in case you know of any positions that I might be a strong fit for — thanks!'

You need to know what you want out of a situation, and you need to know how that person can help. If you are reaching out to someone hoping that *they'll* know how they can help, you've probably already lost the sale. People want to help you. But people are just people, not superheroes or mind readers. Keep these four tips in mind as you work through Steps 6–8:

1. **Keep your opening message short and relevant.**
    Nobody needs your life story today. Remember what you learned from the CV and cover letter lessons? Your job is to give someone just enough context for them to determine who you are, why you're emailing, and whether or not they should care. Heed this warning seriously.

    Imagine you're at an elegant dinner party. You go to shake hands with the stranger seated next to you. When you ask for their name, they do not give it. Instead, they choose to regale you with a seven-paragraph monologue about how they weren't totally sure that this was even the right dinner party for them to attend, and it's probably because they felt wronged by their most recent employer, and they'd recently considered moving to Hong Kong but then their relationship went through a rocky patch and …

… yeah, no. Don't do this.

If you really want a word count limit for networking emails: 85–100 words, max.

2. **Do not falter.**

Even if you're not sure that XYZ career path is the perfect choice for you, please act like it is when you are talking to people in that field. You might surprise yourself and realise you're more interested in this kind of work than you thought you were. You are also much less likely to get a response if your opening line is, 'I'm not sure if I even want this, but …'

3. **Go in for the ask.**

Always get as specific as possible with what you want from this person. If you have no idea what you want from this person, you should hold off on approaching them until you do know.

Remember that this person cannot save you. They cannot read your mind. They are not going to be the Mr Warbucks to your Orphan Annie. They are not some knight in shining armour who will decide on a whim that you, a stranger, appear to be that special person they've been looking to hire. This person will not be able to simultaneously reveal and fulfil your one true dream job. They might, however, respond generously to a well-crafted email from a stranger.

Instead of asking someone if you can 'pick their brain', here are some more concrete ideas:

- Will you tell me what someone with your role actually does day-to-day?

- Could I come shadow you in your office for an afternoon?
- Will you give me 10 minutes' worth of feedback on my CV? Would a company like yours ever hire me? If not, what can I do to change that?
- Do I have the right skills for your position yet? Which skill would you recommend I focus on improving this month in order to become a more attractive candidate?
- Do I absolutely need to go back to school first in order to get this kind of job?
- Will you review my portfolio and tell me which is my weakest example?

4. **Set the other person up for a Yes or No response.**
   You are always asking, more or less, for 20 minutes of someone's time — whether that's them talking on the phone with you, or writing an email back to answer your question, or introducing you to one of their contacts.

   Make it as simple as possible for somebody to agree to, schedule, and show up. Here are some solid etiquette rules to follow:

- Provide a list of time slot choices in your original email.
- Suggest virtual meetings as opposed to in-person ones.
- If you are lucky enough to meet in person, it is your responsibility to travel to their office or location of choice — don't ever ask them to come to you. Ever.
- Always send a calendar invite, so that your appointment is safely secured.

Step 6: Approaching the people you already know

Many of us are quick to brush past our family and friends during the job search because we're either embarrassed to ask for help or we assume they don't have any connections that could directly get us hired. Leaving these people out of the process — the people who should, theoretically, want to see you win the most — is a handicap we give ourselves for no good reason. Stop doing it.

Identifying the right people

Your first mission is to remember who you know in the first place, because I guarantee it's many more people than you realise.

Think through every social group in your life. Who seems well connected, or potentially well connected, in any kind of way? Of the people you know right now, whose career path do you admire? Don't forget:

- Your immediate family
- Your extended family
- Your siblings' friends
- Your friends' siblings
- School friends
- University friends
- Former housemates
- Former colleagues

The connection might not be obvious, so you need to really take a fine-toothed comb to this process and do some thinking. Maybe they live in the city you want to work in. Maybe they used to live in the city you want to work in. Maybe they once mentioned they have a cousin who works in the field you want to work in. Maybe they are just the kind of person who just always seems to be doing something more interesting than everybody else is. Remember that, according to the theory of weak ties, these people do not need to be your closest friends.

PAUSE

Time yourself for 20 minutes a day, every day this week. Think through your friendship groups, scroll through your social media accounts, look at your phone contacts. Come up with a list of 10 people who you think might be able to help, and write down, as specifically as possible, what they might be able to do/answer in order to help you.

You won't come up with a definitive list all at once — even with a fitness plan like mine, networking is still about the imperfect and ever-morphing art of social connection. Your goal is to strike the balance between knowing what you want and letting serendipity dance into your life. Your friend will introduce you to their cousin. Your list will grow.

This list should be enough to get you thinking. *Now that you mention it, I forgot about my friend Amir. He might be a good person to ping about this.* Or, alternatively, you aren't sold yet. *I still don't know anyone relevant. I'm not from that kind of family. I don't know anyone who does what I want to do or works for the companies I want to work for. I am alone on this earth.*

Okay, okay, fine, you're alone. Let's try another strategy. Once you become an adult, it can be easy to forget the communities that made you who you are. You moved away from your home town after school. You graduated from university. It's been years since you thought about that summer club. It's natural to discount those parts of your life as over and done, but I urge you to reconsider. Don't spiral into regret about all the people you failed to keep in touch with over the years, we don't have time for that today. The power of community is not to be underestimated.

Off the top of my head, here are some of the tribes I could tap into at any moment:

- *People who went to my university.*
- *People who went to my school.*
- *People from San Diego also living abroad.*
- *People who have family ties to Las Vegas.*
- *People who identify as musicians and work in office jobs.*
- *The Berlin tech community, the European tech community, the London tech community, the Leeds tech community, the San Francisco tech community, the Chicago tech community, the women-in-tech community.*
- *People who can also sing the whole* Sister Act 2 *medley, a capella.*

I hope you catch my drift. My tribes can all be traced back to specific parts of my life that define me in a strong way — even if it's not a purely professional tie. Yours might be a religion, a football team, a language you grew up speaking. Think of something that bonds you instantly to other people, even strangers, who have that thing in common with you. Something that evokes a feeling of nostalgia that takes you back to a certain place in time.

Marily, who now works at Google, had a great story to share:

Over 10 years ago, I got into World of Warcraft (the online MMORPG game) and I joined a guild focused on coordinating group quests, raids, levelling, etc. The guild had some in-person meet-ups, so I went, I met someone there, and we got to be friends. At some point, she asked me to send her my CV, and, long story short, she got me an interview which eventually landed me my first 'real' job at a startup — a job I really liked! Who knew where gaming can take you.

Remember, your people genuinely want to help you — but nobody can help you if you don't mention that you're looking for a job in the first place.

I want you to take time to really think through your broader communities, because it *is* about who you know — you might just not realise you know them yet! Throughout the entire job search, you should always keep a lookout for your kindred tribes.

Outreach techniques

There are three techniques you can use for approaching your direct network: 1. The public announcement, 2. The board of directors email, and 3. The direct ask.

The public announcement

Why not kickstart your new life as a professional hustler extraordinaire with a grand public announcement to your friends and family? Pick your favourite social platform — honestly, any of them will do — and go take your shot.

If the concept of doing this terrifies you, I want you to repeat after me: *I am proud of myself for looking for a job. There is no shame in telling people what I want out of my career. I am so awesome and brave for putting myself out there. I am making it easy for people to help me and for opportunity to find me.*

The main argument I'll give you for using this tactic that you really cannot predict who is going to know someone who can help you. That childhood friend you haven't spoken to in years might be the one to pull through here, and you wouldn't have remembered (or even known) to text them.

To manage your expectations about public announcements, remember that you don't always see every post from every single one of your friends online. This is not a one-time silver bullet, it's just a way to expand your reach. You still need to follow up specifically with the people you already know will be able to help you.

Public announcement #ENTRYLEVELBOSS template

Friends! Big life news: I am moving to Stockholm at the end of this month and the job search has officially begun. I'm actively look-ing for full-time business development manager roles, and the dream is to work for a cleantech startup (something like Company X or Company Y if you know the industry!) that specialises in sustainable city planning.

If you have friends or contacts in Stockholm, I ask that you please introduce me! I am actively on the hunt for this next professional adventure … and also for killer cinnamon buns …

My LinkedIn: [insert URL]

My email: [insert email]

DM me if you might be able to help, and I'm happy to send over an email with more details.

The board of directors email

If making a big announcement feels too extroverted (or maybe you have a full-time job you haven't left yet and need to be discreet), you could consider the board of directors email approach.

What's a board of directors? According to investopedia.com, a board of directors is 'a group of individuals elected to represent shareholders. A board's mandate is to establish policies for corporate management and oversight, making decisions on major company issues. Every public company must have a board of directors.'

Repurposed for our needs, it's a select group of advisors from a few different chapters of your own life. They aren't your best friends, they're your best mentors. You likely admire their professional trajectory, even if it's not the exact path you want to pursue for yourself. This dozen-ish people could be comprised of former professional contacts (maybe a favourite ex-boss), mentors (maybe a babysitter or family friend or professor), friends (maybe a university housemate who always gave great advice), or family members (maybe the smartest of your cousins).

Ideally, it's a mix of people who know you in a professional capacity and people who are always rooting for you, all of whom might be well positioned to help you. The further into your career you get, the more and more this group will be comprised of your favourite ex-colleagues or professional contacts.

Put everybody on BCC so that you don't rope all these people that don't know each other into a Reply All disaster.

The most important thing to remember when writing this email — and almost any other email you send throughout this process — is that it could possibly be forwarded to someone who could hire you. Always write for that audience.

Board of directors email #ENTRYLEVELBOSS template

Subject line: *Big life news from me*

To my wisest mentors,
You're receiving this email because I consider you to be on my personal board of directors. And because I value your life/career advice, I want to tell you that I am (quietly and actively) on the hunt for a new job ... in Cambridge!
Yep, I'm moving at the end of this month so that Julian and I can finally live in the same place again. And while I'm going to miss Devon cream teas more than anything, I am excited about this new chapter.
Job-wise, I am actively looking for a full-time role:
- A junior-level non-specialist NHS jobs, like healthcare assistant
- Based in Cambridge, of course
- Happily reporting for duty as soon as 8 June!

The dream is to work for a large hospital. The work I've been doing as a receptionist at my local GP surgery this year is definitely applicable, and I really want to continue working in healthcare.

If you have friends or professional contacts in Cambridge, I want to meet them. Will you please introduce me or pass on my name? I'm working hard to schedule as many meetings and phone interviews as I can ahead of landing, so that I can hit the ground running.

My LinkedIn: [insert URL]

CV: Attached!

Happy to give you more specifics. Please let me know how I can make it easy for you. Regardless, wish me luck and come visit us in Cambridge. And thank you for always having my back.

The direct ask

Every so often, you're going to know exactly how somebody could help you.

I promise you, whether it's your oldest friend or a distant childhood acquaintance, this person just wants you to ask them what they already know you want to ask them. I know it's hard to be straightforward about this stuff. I know it can feel like you're bothering this person. But trust me: it's much more awkward to be on the receiving end of communication from somebody in your personal life who wants something from you professionally but appears to be too nervous to come out and ask for it directly.

Also, if somebody offers to help before you even ask them, please don't waste their time (or your own) by being shy and telling them you don't need help. You do need help. Take them up on their offer as soon as you're ready, whether it's an introduction or a reference. Help them to help you. Always make it as easy as possible, even when it's a friend.

Direct ask #ENTRYLEVELBOSS template

Subject line: *Looking for a little help!*

Hey [First Name],

How are things? I stalked the honeymoon photos last month and Greece looks delightful.

Getting in touch with some big life news: I'm moving to Melbourne! My boyfriend lives there and we're stupidly excited to be in the same place again.

I'm in full-on job search mode in the lead-up to the move, and I noticed that you used to work for Company X in the Sydney office. They're one of the employers I'd really like to talk to in Melbourne (I have my heart set on fundraising for a performing arts or music foundation).

Do you know happen to anybody in that office? Or anybody in Sydney who still works at the company? I haven't found a perfect position posted on the Careers page ... but from my stalking/research, I think it makes the most sense for me to chat with someone on the fundraising and development team.

If you have any related suggestions or thoughts, I'm all ears. Thanks so much in advance if you can help!

Thanks,

X

PS: Attaching a CV and my LinkedIn in case the stars align and you can pass it along. THANK YOU AGAIN!

Warning: don't be this person

The biggest pitfall you'll succumb to with this kind of networking is forgetting to do your professional research about the people you know in a personal context. You may know your friends or friends of friends in drinks mode, but now you're about to ask for a professional favour. You need to give the people you know the same respect that you'd give to a stranger. This might sound obvious, so let me please put the fear of God into you for a minute.

As we know, I'm a San Diego native who has muscled her way into both the United Kingdom and Germany several times: study visas, work visas, fancier work visas, bureaucracy, a lot of paperwork. When it comes to immigration law in western Europe, I really know the ropes. I am a vast well of very specific and very helpful knowledge. Because of this, I get hit up all the time by friends who have friends who want to move from America to Europe (or the other way around).

I want to tell you about a time this went really wrong, a few years back, when a mutual friend introduced over me over Facebook Messenger to a friend of hers. The friend of a friend was an American woman, my age, who was thinking about moving to Berlin because her UK study visa was about to run out. I told her I was happy to get on the phone for 20 minutes and answer questions.

'Thanks in advance!' she replied. 'I will hit you up soon!'

Okay, ball in her court. All good.

About a week later, I was doing a routine check through my Facebook message requests, and I spotted a new message from this friend-of-a-friend woman. This was her first mistake. She didn't add me on Facebook, so I basically found her message by luck. If she had responded on that same conversation thread (the one our mutual friend started), I would have seen her message immediately.

Slightly edited, here's what that message said:

hey alexa how's it goingggg?? basically i'm intrigued at your move to germany and exit from the uk … firstly, i don't really think there is any way i can stay here, but did you almost find one? i heard you might have. also, when you moved to germany, did you instantly start your own work as in working for yourself? also do you speak german? i'm just curious as to how that transition worked for you, let me know when you get a spare moment. thanks! Xo

No. No, no, no, no, no.

I remember reading this message and banging my head against the wall. Oh, honey. You fool! You had the chance to get very solid advice on a subject that very few people know about, for free, from the perfect person, from the best weak tie you were likely to find, and you went and shot yourself in the foot.

Later that week, I made a big fat list of all the reasons she screwed up. I put them in the #ENTRYLEVELBOSS newsletter, which I'm sure this woman never read, even though she would have known about said newsletter had she bothered to look me up for even five seconds. Brace yourself, reader, because this turns sassy pretty quickly. But perhaps I've been a bit too encouraging in my tone so far, and I'm guessing that someone out there needs to hear this.

So, without further ado, I'll repeat it for you here …

Girl, you do not know me.
I appreciate that I am approximately your same age and that we share a good friend in common. This does not give you an excuse to:
Use this much casual punctuation.
Use a boatload of incorrect, informal grammar.

Not introduce yourself or give me context in any way, shape, or form.

Not even capitalise my name???

I don't know what you know about me, but please do your research. I am a professional business owner who already offered to get on the phone with you for 20 minutes to try to help.

Here are the answers to the questions you actually asked me: Good, Yes, Yes, Poorly.

'i'm just curious as to how that transition worked for you' is not a question. It is a poorly phrased statement about your own curiosity. No, I am not going to sit down and write you a five-paragraph essay on my entire life history, on how I moved to Berlin sight unseen at age 25, on how I started my business from scratch, on how I got my first clients. If you googled me, which you did not, you would see that I've written more than one article on these topics. You would know that I didn't actually move from the UK to Germany, as you seem to be assuming, but that I spent an intense year in San Francisco in-between. You would see that I write a newsletter read by thousands of people. And maybe, just maybe, you would have come at me in a different way.

I am not going to let you know 'when I get a spare moment'.

I already told you, let's talk on the phone.

I will take 20 minutes out of my day and give them to you. I will tell you my life story, and explain how I did it all, and cheer you on, and tell you I'm happy to introduce you to people when you get to town. I will do that because our mutual friend is flipping fantastic, and she cares about you, and I care about her. You should have come back to me the first time and said, 'Awesome. Thank you. Are you free sometime on Tuesday between 10am and 4pm UK time? Let me know what number to call you at, and I'll take care of the rest.'

Insert yourself into my calendar. I already invited you to do so. But, Lord, do not ask me to find a spare moment and then come back to check with *you* if my sacred extra moment works for *your* schedule. Nah, baby, we ain't doing it like that.

… but I didn't say any of that to her. Instead, I'm saying it to you, dear reader, so that you never get yourself into this situation ever. Ever. E-v-e-r, do you hear me?

I did reply to her message, for the record. I said:

> Hey, good to hear from you. Easiest to chat on the phone so I can answer all your questions straight away. I'm around tonight or tomorrow. Just ping me and we can chat.

> Seen, but never got a response.

As it has been said a billion times before, you never get a second chance to make a first impression. Keep your tone friendly, but demonstrate your professionalism early and often.

Step 6 task list

1. **Brainstorm your way through all your personal and professional circles.** If it helps, start with a list of tribes (high school! Netball friends!) first and then move on to people. The number doesn't matter today. Think as broadly and creatively as you can — people can surprise you.
2. **Pick a person, pick a template, and craft your own email.** The first one will be the hardest. Tomorrow's email will come more easily.

Step 7: Approaching the companies you want to work for

When I was 17, I wanted to get in to the University of Notre Dame more than anything in the world. I did well in school, but didn't have the highest grade in the class. No one in my family had ever gone to Notre Dame, so I was never going to be a legacy student. I had never played a varsity sport, which apparently is a big deal. But none of that fazed me. I was *going* to Notre Dame. And I was going to email every professor and every admissions counsellor and everyone I'd ever met who had a second cousin who'd ever even *heard* of Notre Dame until the entire world agreed with me.

---

4 January 2007
Subject line: *ND Alexa Shoen*

Mr D,

Happy New Year, I hope you are having a good January! We spoke a few months back about the jazz vocalist programme at Notre Dame. I sent in my audition CD on 26 December, and as you instructed, titled it 'Jazz Vocalist Audition' so that it was sent to you and not to a classical vocal instructor. I do not know how long it takes for supplements to be logged in under the Golden

Dome, but hopefully you will be receiving my CD soon!

You also told me back in November that it was not necessary to come out to South Bend in person to audition because those dates on the website were for classical vocalists. Of course the weather is significantly more pleasant here in San Diego, but I feel very strongly that I come across best in live performance and would love to discuss a possible future role in the jazz programme with you. I'd really love to see the ensembles perform, too.

I realise this may not be possible, especially because you are gearing up for your spring concert tour and whatnot, but if it is, please know that I want to do so. Also, if you would be inclined to request a repertoire list or musical CV, I have those on file. Thanks so much for your time and consideration.

Warmest regards,

Alexa Shoen

I was a 17-year-old #ENTRYLEVELBOSS, hustling to the best of my 17-year-old abilities. And, by being relentless in pursuit of what I wanted and letting myself ask for help over and over again, I managed to pull it off.

I vividly remember the day I got my acceptance letter. First, I fell down on the floor crying. And then I emailed the admissions counsellor I'd befriended eight months previously when he came to visit my school, and whom I'd been emailing back and forth with weekly ever since. 'Alexa, I was waiting for this email,' he wrote back to me. 'I wanted to tell you so badly as soon as I found out. You are IN!!! Welcome to Notre Dame.'

Could my grades and extra-curricular activities have been more impressive? Probably. But did I put in the best application humanly possible for Notre Dame, and then make sure they knew my name and understood my strengths and that I absolutely would not give up until they let me in? Yes. (And was I just as worthy of being there as all of my classmates, even though my grades might not have been as high as theirs? Also yes.)

Some companies will be rigid about their application processes. If there are explicit rules, abide by them. I've seen a few application pages that say 'No phone calls about this position', for example. Part of having a job is about following directions and listening — and at the end of the day, that part is just as important as being passionate about the work.

But if you can reach out, in addition to submitting the best application possible, do it. Just do it. And if you ever run into somebody who is truly bothered by you reaching out, especially if there was no explicit request not to do so on their website? I call bad vibes. I say we take our business some place else. I mean, honestly, if a candidate really wants to come work for you, goes through the effort of submitting an application, and then you decide you want to ding them for taking the initiative to come tell you how badly they want to help your company grow? You deserve to lose that candidate to another company.

Identifying the right people

First, look for anyone who could maybe make a warm introduction on your behalf:

1. **Take your Target Employer List and head over to LinkedIn.**
    If you don't have that many connections on LinkedIn yet, this won't work as well — but try it out anyway. You might be surprised by what you find!
2. **Type each company name into the search bar and hit enter.**
    You'll see a list of people who work there, with all your 1st and 2nd connections listed at the top.
    1st Connections = people you are connected to on LinkedIn
    2nd Connections = where the magic happens
    You might have a 1st Connection who works at one of your target employers (or used to work there) — that would be a pretty lucky situation. But the odds are much higher that you see at least a few 2nd Connections at these employers. This means you are one degree of separation away from your destiny! You have a mutual friend.
3. **Use the techniques from Step 5 to approach this mutual friend.** Ask for an introduction to the 2nd Connection person.
4. **Keep going through the list of employees.** Make a list of anybody who looks like they could be helpful. You might already have this list started from when you put together your Target Employer List (see page 46). If you're using the free version of LinkedIn, you might only be able to see a partial list of employees.

Don't go straight for the CEO or the head of the department unless it's a small company of 150 employees or fewer. The closer you can get to the people who would actually become your future co-workers, the better. These people will be more likely to respond to you because you could potentially directly impact their day-to-day life. They can offer valuable advice, too, since they probably know personally what it takes to get hired into your position.

Don't only focus your attention on finding the recruiters or HR people at your target employer — unless you yourself want to be a recruiter, of course! Instead, I want you to look for: 1. Peers at your same-ish seniority level who work inside the relevant department, or 2. People who look like they might be the hiring manager for the kind of role you would want. For example, if you want to be a sales assistant, be on the look-out for other sales assistants, the sales managers, or the sales lead.

That being said, if your goal is to go work for a large company — the kind that employs a whole team of in-house recruiters to find talent — don't be afraid to introduce yourself to those people on LinkedIn. Mary, a lead recruiter for Facebook, says many recruiters would be happy to hear from you: 'My whole job is to source great candidates. If you can introduce yourself, link me to your portfolio, and tell me which of our positions you'd be suited to, you're ultimately making my life (and the life of any recruiter) easier.'

I'll add my own two cents: most recruiters will be tasked with sourcing talent for a company's more senior roles, so this might not be your best plan of attack for an entry-level job. Regardless, make sure you're reaching out to someone who actually recruits for your kind of position. I wouldn't go to Mary, who focuses on technology roles, if I wanted a job in sales, for example.

> **TIP**
> Only reach out to one person at a time, per company. You never know who sits next to each other in the office. Contacting everybody at once will look like spam. (If you don't get a response from the first person right away, be patient. If a week goes by, follow up. If following up doesn't work, consider taking a new approach or moving on to the next person.)

How to actually find contact information for these people

You look at their profile. You google them. You look them up on Twitter and Instagram. You try to find a personal website. You get curious and you keep digging around the internet. You check the website for a team photos page. You straight-up guess at their email address and see if you're right. You keep trying. As if you're trying to find a way to contact the person your best friend met in Ibiza — the one who might possibly be the love of her life. You try that hard.

I have slid into many a DM for professional purposes, but you should use your best judgement to decide how to approach each person on your list. You might find a public Twitter or Instagram profile, or a professional website or LinkedIn page that lists their email address. You might make an educated guess about their email address based on seeing another employee's email address. It will be different for every situation.

> **ETIQUETTE TIP**
> Remember that these people are all humans who have their own hopes and dreams and, importantly, their own lives outside of work. Do not hire a private detective or do anything creepy that would make this person fear for their life or their safety. You want to get hired, not arrested.

What to do if there's a role online

Apply before you reach out. Put in a killer application as soon as humanly possible, using all the prep work you did in Part 2 to help you make it sparkle. The reason I want you to apply *before* you make contact is so that you can avoid the following situation:

> **You:** Hello! I'm X! I want to work for you!
> **Them:** Hi, that's great. Have you filled out an application yet?
> **You:** Oh. Uhh, no. You're right, there is one on your Careers page. I'll … umm, I'll come back to you next week …

Submitting applications is no longer against the rules. You're prepared now, remember? This is healthy applying, not job-search junk-food diet applying. If there is a role you want at a company you like, you have my permission to go for it with all your might. Follow their rules, play their game, go forth and submit an application.

A lot of companies will need you to submit an application in order to start interviewing you, even if you get the interview through a personal connection.

Applying also just shows you're willing to put in the work. We want to strike a balance between following the rules for your target employer's application process and demonstrating clearly that you really want *this* particular job at this particular company.

#ENTRYLEVELBOSS template

If there is a role online, but you've never met this person:

Hi [Potential Colleague],
You don't know me yet, but I'm [Your Name], and I just submitted

an application for the [Job I Want] position this morning.

I wanted to send over a quick note to you directly, because coming to work for [Company X] is my number one professional priority. [Here's an additional specific thing about why I really want to be your colleague, and here's a reference to why I'm such a good fit for this role.]

Just introducing myself and letting you know how genuinely excited I am about the opportunity. No need to respond, but I'd love the chance to speak with you about the role once the application gets processed. Have a wonderful weekend!

Warmly,

[Your Name]

If there is a role online and you've met this person before: (FYI, this is the exact LinkedIn message I sent to two future colleagues at Facebook!)

Hey John, hey Natalie,

Happy New Year to you both! We met at the October Content Strategy event.

I've officially made the move over to London from Berlin, and it looks like you guys are now conveniently hiring for new Content Strategists. Wanted to let you know that I just submitted my application.

Would love to come in for a coffee sometime soon, either way!

Good vibes,

Alexa

PS: Please let Alex know I tried to write 'chops' under the Skills section and it wouldn't let me.

What to do if there's no role online

I've seen way too many people cross their dream company off their Target Employer List because they didn't happen to see a job posting listed on the day they checked. Don't give up so easily! We must retain our optimism and relentlessly chase our dreams, people. Always assume that your target employer is either 1. hiring right now, or 2. definitely will be soon.

So, introduce yourself, pitch your skillset, take your shot. Do not leave opportunity on the table just because some company's Careers page was out of date. I meet people every single week who want to excitedly tell me about the off-the-menu jobs they got — the ones that never made it onto the internet. Here are a couple of examples:

> I messaged the director of operations of a workout studio
> I was obsessed with, where I'd previously attended a few
> classes. The company did not have a Careers page on their
> website — but I looked at the studio website, saw that she
> was the closest thing to an HR manager, went to LinkedIn,
> and messaged her. Even though there weren't any listed
> openings, I decided to try anyway. I introduced myself and
> asked if they were looking for any front desk support. I
> wound up getting an interview and an offer!
>
> *Avalon, Orange County*

I recently cold-emailed a designer at a company I would love to work at, which led to an interview. I picked this particular woman because she'd worked with people I knew at a previous company. I scoped her portfolio and socials to get a sense of her personality, so I knew what kind of tone to take in the email. She seemed fun and bright — and honestly had a VERY cool haircut — so I thought it would be okay to approach her casually. I introduced myself, explained that I knew her through so-and-so from that other company, and told her that I had just moved back to Pittsburgh. I said I had always admired her company's work, that I use their product personally, and that I had been working for a company in the same industry for the last three years.

I quickly outlined what a normal day of responsibilities looks like for me, and asked if that sounded anywhere near what a typical day looks like for her. I ended with: 'If these sound like tasks your team would need help with, I would love to know about any open positions. If not, would you be open to meeting up and chatting more about some other areas I could grow in to maybe be a fit on your team in the future?' She replied and cc'd their VP of design and just said that those tasks are exactly what they need help with, and that this VP would love to meet with me the following week! I think people are usually more open when you have ANY kind of connection you can draw to them, even if it's something as simple as 'I admire you and your company's work.'

Jenelle, Pittsburgh

I have an English literature degree and a diploma in screenwriting. After I finished my diploma I was tinkering with some screen stuff but getting impatient so I decided to try making radio documentaries (since I was listening to so many podcasts) and, with the help of a few people, taught myself how to do that. I made a few documentaries for community radio and then pitched one to a national radio network and got picked up. I ended up making three docs for them before I got asked to do a five-week fill-in gig producing daily radio for an arts program. I got on-the-job training and have been at the network ever since and have now become a digital producer, again informally learning how to write articles on the job. Only in the last month did they formally advertise my job; I applied and I've been made permanent.

Hannah, Melbourne

I always incorrectly assumed that, if the kind of role you want isn't listed, they won't hire you — until I got an internship somewhere that didn't say they were looking for interns. I introduced myself to the CEO and convinced him to take me on. I didn't think this was possible until I tried it for myself.

Finlay, London

#ENTRYLEVELBOSS Template

For the 'Hi, I want to come and work for you' email:

Hi [Potential Colleague],

You don't know me yet, but I'm [Your Name], an account manager who's relocating from Bristol to Liverpool next month.

I'm getting in touch because I'm actively on the hunt for a new role and [Company X] is exactly the kind of employer I'm looking for — an innovative digital-first talent agency that understands brand-building for the influencer generation. Finally!

I wanted to reach out to you, specifically, because I've been working on [a relevant project I'm doing for my current employer] over the last year, and [this is how I see it making your company some money or saving your company some time].

I have no idea what your team's hiring plans are like for the next few months, but I wanted to introduce myself regardless and let you know how excited I was to learn about the company.

If there's a role opening up soon, I would love to apply. And even if not, I would love to meet up for a coffee during the first week of June, if you'd be game to give a Liverpool newbie the lay of the land. Let me know!

Warmly,

[Your Name]

For the 'Hi, I want to come work for you' DM on social media:

Hey [Potential Colleague],

You don't know me, but I'm [Your Name], an account manager moving from Bristol to Liverpool next month. Ever so slightly embarrassed about the shady DM, but I'm actively on the hunt for a new role and [Company X] is 100% my dream job. So … hello!

No clue what your team's hiring plans are like for the next few months, but I wanted to introduce myself regardless. Would you be open to connecting? If you shoot over your email address, I can follow up there.

[Your Name]

Step 7 task list

1. **Find three to four contacts for each company on your Target Employer List.** You should only reach out to one person at a time, but it's always good to have a few options.
2. **Do the required detective work to find email addresses or contact information.** Use your best judgement — but, also, get creative. Google your way through it.
3. **Pick a person, pick a template, craft your own email.** Focus on nailing your introductory elevator pitch. Remember that this person has no context for you. What do they need to know in order to email you back? There is no singular perfect answer. Your elevator pitch, just like your CV, will shapeshift based on your audience.

Step 8: Approaching the Magical Sparks

'Alexa, I'm at the end of all my lists. Nobody I know can help me. And, yes, I messaged somebody at every single target employer — except for the ones where I couldn't find any contact information. Nobody ever got back to me. This whole thing didn't work. I'm going back to just sending in lots of applications and playing the numbers game.'

The first thing I ever promised you, way back at the beginning of this book, was that there will always be a next step you can take. I know that the dead ends can start to leave a bitter taste in your mouth after a while. (I'd like to make an argument that it's actually a really good sign if you're getting a little bummed out every now and again, because it means you're chasing opportunities that you truly find interesting, but I know that can feel like a poor consolation prize if this process starts dragging on for longer than you expected.)

It does not feel good when you want to keep cruising, but look down to find that your petrol tank — in this case, the list of contacts to chase down — is running dangerously low. Well, fear not, friend. You know that I always have a plan.

In a moment like this, we can shift gears into Magical Spark networking mode. Magical Spark networking is my favourite of all the networking tactics because you basically get to go out into the world, sprinkle pixie dust everywhere, and watch things transform into technicolour right before your very eyes. It's like realising that Hogwarts exists.

Magical Sparks are, in short, the strangers that can turn your world upside down. Whether that's the person who asked a smart question at the event you attended this morning, the smiling face you took note of while scrolling through LinkedIn, or the person you've been bantering with on Twitter for the last six months — they all fit into the same category. These are the accidental and intentional connections that people like to make movies about. These are the human moments that make the world go round if you're willing to let (or make) them happen.

If you take away anything from Step 8, let it be this: it is never too late to be the type of person who knows the right people because, in my experience, the 'right' people are constantly out there asking questions and meeting new people all the time. Very, very, very few humans on this planet were born into a social circle so elite that they shook hands with all their future business contacts on the playground and never had to make a new friend after the age of 13. I know it can feel like that's how it works, but you'd be surprised. The possibilities of Magical Spark networking offer us a prime example of a way in which the internet has democratised access to opportunity.

You have the power to go meet new people any time you like. The most professionally impressive people I know are doing this all of the time. Weekly, in fact. Even when they don't need a new job. They catch lectures on Tuesday nights because they want to learn something new. They follow up and grab coffee with someone they happened to meet at their cousin's wedding. They DM each other on Monday mornings and say, 'Hi. I'm so-and-so and I do such-and-such and right now I'm super stuck. Do you know how to do X? Or do you know anyone who knows how? My plan so far has been to stumble my way through — but I must be missing a trick. Can you point me in the right direction?'

Bo Ren (who I met on Twitter and then finally grabbed drinks with years later) puts it this way: 'Professionally grabbing coffee with smart people is a skill. Knowing how to establish a genuine connection, presenting yourself authentically, and asking good questions is a skill that comes with practice. These coffees do add up in multiplicity.'

Whether this connection turns into a long-term mentorship or not is beside the point. Sometimes you just need to go hunt down a stranger who seems to have their shit together more than you do and — with the right amount of hubris and humour — ask them to give it to you straight. I equate this practice with the sensation of sticking your head around the heavy velvet curtain and finding somebody backstage who can pass you an extra safety pin so that your costume doesn't come apart at the seams. Everybody knows the show needs to go on — you'll be surprised how many people will conspire to help you keep dancing. (They've all been there, too.)

William, from Washington DC, shared this crazy story with me:

One day in university I cold-emailed Philip Mudd, the former deputy director of the Counter Terrorism Center at the CIA and deputy director at the FBI under Robert Mueller, after reading about him in a magazine. He said people hate on him all the time, so I shot him a quick thank-you note to balance out the hate. Anyways, he called me three days later while I was walking out of class. He asked me about myself and what I wanted to do with my life. I was just like, 'Philip Mudd, from the CIA and FBI, that Philip Mudd?' He told me to send him my CV at the end of the call.

It never went any further than that, but it was still probably the coolest thing that's ever happened to me.

A friend once explained this as the practice of throwing serendipity bombs out into the universe, just to see what might happen. Strange, how the universe likes to reward us for such things.

Identifying the right people

You've got two choices:

1. Physically going out into the world and letting serendipity find you.
2. Googling your way around the internet to find someone awesome.

Beyond that, there are no rules. You should approach the people you always assumed were unapproachable. You should treat every person you encounter as if they might secretly be holding the key to your dream job — because, for all you know, they are.

Where to start if you don't know where to start (in person)

It's possible to work your way through the entirety of an #ENTRYLEVELBOSS job search without ever leaving your house, but sometimes going out into the world and letting serendipity smack you in the face is exactly what the doctor ordered. I especially recommend offline networking when you're trying to decide between industries, re-spark your motivation, or get more information about a new field. In person, you'll come across people that you wouldn't have known how to locate on the internet.

There are a thousand ways to find professional events happening in your local area. The key, as always, is to get specific and be strategic with your search. You aren't just looking for 'networking events in Los Angeles' anymore. You know what you want and what your keywords are — so go find your thing! Do some browsing for public events on Eventbrite and Facebook. Check out the upcoming public lectures schedule at your local university or library. You don't necessarily need to spend a ton of money on a conference ticket. You could, however, offer to volunteer at an event or festival or conference. Boom bam pow, free entry.

Christina, an American based in Mexico City, tried the conference volunteer route for her most recent job search:

I couldn't afford the ticket, so I applied to be a volunteer, and then strategically chose my hours on the day before or outside of conference hours, so that I could attend the conference full-time. I downloaded the attendee spreadsheet in advance and did some deep stalking. I 'Ctrl-F'-ed my way through it, looking for anyone with a title associated with the kind of role I wanted. I contacted a whole bunch of people in the days leading up to the event, asking for just 5–10 minutes in person to learn about their career path and how they put the pieces together for themselves. Most didn't respond. Of the ones who did, one person agreed to have coffee with me first thing in the morning on the last day. We had a good but brief chat about her career. Then, about a month later, she actually wound up leaving her job … and she put my name forward as her replacement. Because we had met, and she had context on me, the team approached me and encouraged me to apply. And now I'm the head of investor relations!

TIP
Make the most of every Q&A opportunity. Ask your most thoughtful question to the speaker — but remember to introduce yourself to the audience, too! Dr Christian Busch, a professor who teaches on serendipity at New York University, refers to this as the practice of dropping conversational 'hooks' into the world. If you give others something specific to latch on to, they might see a connection you couldn't have predicted. They may approach *you*. If you include some context in your question, someone else can come and talk to you about it after

the session ends.

Example: 'As someone who just recently moved here from San Diego …'

Example: 'I'm currently teaching myself Photoshop, and …'

Example: 'I just read [some book], and it made me see that …'

Example: 'I'm the first university graduate in my family, and …'

TIP

Keep your eyes open at all times. You can use that same tactic of dropping 'hooks' into conversation any time, not exclusively at professional events. I once coached a student who ultimately landed a job through a person he met at his friend's grandmother's funeral. When people casually ask you what you do, tell them what you *want* to do. Tell them about your future.

TIP

Arrive alone and a little bit too early, on purpose. When you're the first one to show up at an event, the organisers will be excited to greet you and start a conversation. As more people arrive, the organiser will usually introduce you to the next guest so that they can excuse themselves to get back to dealing with the event logistics. Now, even if you don't make a single other friend, you've met the most connected person at the event (the organiser) and at least a couple other early-arriving comrades.

Where to start if you don't know where to start (online)

If you're really stuck and have no clue who you'd want to talk to in your industry, start by googling your way towards people who are doing interesting and market-leading work in your home town (or desired new home town). Don't get overwhelmed and think you need to reach out to celebrities. Think local. Look for the people in your own backyard who have already put in the work to become part of the business community that you are trying to tap into. As a start, you could google stuff like:

- Business awards Wellington
- Young leaders Oklahoma City
- Top property lawyer Cardiff
- Brewery owners Kent
- Best UX designers Montreal

You could also look for people who have job titles similar to the ones you are seeking, but at companies you might not want to work for right now.

> **TIP**
> Find the right people by using the hunting techniques you used for Step 7, but instead of going straight to your would-be hiring manager, seek out people who can assess your skillset properly *without* any of the pressure that comes with a real interview situation. These will likely be people five or six years ahead of you in their career path. They are probably working at a company you respect (and would maybe even like to work for) but that isn't your I-would-die-to-interview-there first choice.

One idea: go solicit feedback from smart people

While there's no roadmap for serendipity, I have an example of when Magical Spark networking might be helpful for you.

I once coached a student named Caroline who had gone back to university to get a second degree in computer science, after having started her career in a completely different specialisation. She was about to graduate. While she was really excited about becoming a data scientist, Caroline had no personal connections to anybody who did anything of the sort. Over the course of my own career, I had worked with enough data scientists to roughly assess Caroline's skillset and ask a few questions about her course curriculum, but I didn't know enough, either. Neither one of us were sure whether or not she had enough training to be considered for junior roles.

'We need to go get some opinions from real data scientists,' I told her. This was a perfect situation for Magical Spark networking. We reached out to five data scientists. Three answered her emails, two invited her to their office for coffee, and one explained to her exactly which critical skill she was missing. She taught herself that thing using YouTube tutorials, and then checked back in with her Magical Spark person in order to make sure she had got it right. Within six weeks, she was a fully employed junior data scientist.

Whether you're changing careers, just starting your job search after leaving school or graduating from university, or putting new skills to work for the first time ever: you can do this, too.

Why is reaching out for feedback such a helpful tactic? Two reasons: 1. you get expert opinions from people who already have the job you want, and 2. they might think you're talented and want to put you forward for another job that you don't even know about yet. Score.

#ENTRYLEVELBOSS Template

Hey [Magical Spark],

I'm [Your Name] and I'm about to graduate with a BS in Computer Science this August. After two years in the charity sector, I decided to retrain and I'm now excited to dive headfirst into the tech industry. I know I want to be a data scientist, which is great, but I'm not 100% sure what that actually means for me yet.

Here's where I'm at: I can run basic queries in SQL and, from my charity background, I know I'm most passionate about backing up strong UX decisions with solid data understanding.

I'm reaching out to a couple of seasoned data scientists (like yourself) who work at big-name companies to get a deeper understanding of what the gap is between my current skillset and what I need to start getting hired for paid internships and junior-level DS jobs.

Would you be willing to take 15 minutes on the phone with me next week?

If yes, shoot me your email address and I'll send over a couple time slot ideas. Thank you so, so, so much in advance. I could really use the help.

[Your Name]

Step 8 task list

1. **Decide on your first Magical Spark person.** You could send out one Magical Spark email a day for the rest of your life if you wanted to (and I know a few people out there who do!).

2. **Before you reach out to this person (or the next), pause to answer the following questions:** what do I want from this person? Why do I think this is the right person to answer that question for me? Is there anything else I should try to learn (or google) about this person before I get in touch?

3. **Craft your first Magical Spark email.** Just like with the Step 7 emails, remember that this person has no context for you. Be as specific as you can with your request. Make it stupid-easy for them to say yes.

Part 4

And Now It's Your Turn

'Success is just a series of to-do lists.'
Me, Alexa Shoen, author of this very book

Step 9: Rinse and repeat

At many points over the years that I've spent putting this curriculum together, I have tried to explain exactly what it is that I'm teaching people. Career coaching never felt accurate — mostly because I hate personality tests, and find it unhelpful to plunge yourself deeper into an existential crisis without practical next steps when your rent is due. Personal opinion. Coaching also sometimes implies that you, job seeker, have possessed the answers in your heart all along. As if all you really needed was a moment of self-reflection to think about stuff. That's not it, either. The closest I could ever get was to tell people I had developed a fitness plan for the process of applying for jobs.

What you do with any fitness plan is up to you. You could make every suggested meal once and feel good about the fact that you were mixing it up. You could follow the whole programme for a week and discover that you start sleeping better and that the whites of your eyes look a little brighter. You could pick and choose the parts of the diet that are right for you, making it a little bit easier to be a little bit healthier forever. Or, if you're lucky, you find a diet you can really get behind. One that makes you feel amazing, even on the days when it's hard. It's something that just … makes sense to you. And so you keep going. You live that way, day in and day out, until you look around and realise that you've changed your own life.

By now, you know that there is no secret trick or silver bullet. This is the really annoying thing about fitness plans — they don't work unless you repeat the behaviour over and over again. That's what they're meant for, in fact. They offer a template by which to live your life. I have provided you with a template by which to find your next job (and the one after that, and the one after that).

Of the hundreds of people who read this book before it went to print, several of them were hiring managers or the kind of people that receive a lot of cold emails related to their profession. Every single one of those people said the same thing to me: 'Yeah, this all makes sense. I don't answer every message (I don't have the time!), but the ones who send me messages like this … I tend to answer those much more often.'

I know, down to my bones, that this framework works. I hear it from all the people who have gone before you. But you and I both know that these kinds of processes don't work if you just do every step once, and then sit back and wonder what went wrong. If you send one email, freak out, and give up, I cannot help you.

The more that you repeat the behaviours in this book, the more natural they will become to you. The more comfortable you get with sending the emails, the less scary it will become. The more often you go back to your notes to remember which people you're trying to find and which companies you wanted to work for in the first place, the better off you will be. And soon, if you haven't already, you will find yourself cracking your knuckles and saying to yourself: 'Cool, I want to work for this company on my Target Employer List. I've got a plan, and I'm going to make it happen.' It won't feel scary at all.

At some point very soon, you're going to get your break. You will be working this very system, you'll open your emails, and you'll freeze up because — would you look at that! —you've got a response. I want to leave you with this wonderful story from Amanda, a hiring manager in Chicago:

In the summer of 2018, I was hiring for an entry-level role on my team and we were in a serious time crunch. We had interviewed several candidates and just didn't feel that any of them had the right combination of skillset and fit for our team. Out of the blue, a recent graduate from my university messaged me on LinkedIn asking about a different position, wondering if I would be willing to talk to her about my experience at the company and see if she would be a good fit to refer for the role. I ended up interviewing her and asking her to apply to my team instead. Our team subsequently interviewed her on a Thursday, I offered her the role on Friday, and she started her new job with us on Monday. Sure, sometimes it might not pan out to message strangers and ask for help, but you also might ask the right person the right question at the right time.

Keep going, friend. Work the system. Hone your message, send your emails, shoot your shot. And, on the days that you stumble, come back to me. These lessons will be here as reminders. That's the great thing about writing a book. I'll be here, waiting, whenever you get knocked down. Come back, and we'll start again.

Step 9 task list

1. **Check back through Steps 1–8.** Make a note of any task list items you haven't completed yet.
2. **Spend 45 minutes organising. Then write yourself a game plan.** What can you accomplish this week that will move the needle on your search? Who can you reach out to? Write out a list of steps, but make them all tiny little baby steps. These can be things like 'Track down so-and-so's email address' or 'Make a copy of my CV and tailor it for the _____ application.'

Interview advice

This is a book about everything that happens before the interview.

I wrote all of this down because I wanted to provide, for others, all of the crucial context that I never knew I was missing. During my job searching days, most of the career advice I came across seemed to incorrectly assume that I had already found a way to score the interview. I perceived this as a pretty giant leap to conclusions.

Attending the interview — or the informational interview, or the coffee date, or the whatever — is not the hard part. By putting the tools I've given you to use, you will have got past the hard part. Cutting through the noise, reaching the people you need to reach, explaining in writing why you're the right person to spend an hour with in the first place? That's where this game gets won. That being said, I (obviously) have a few final thoughts on the topic before we part ways.

Confirmations, thank-you notes, and next steps

If I'm a hiring manager and I don't hear anything from a candidate on the day of an interview, I am already planning what I will do with those 45 minutes assuming that they flake on me. I also expect them to follow up the next day to say thanks, that they enjoyed chatting, and that they are clear on the next steps. These might seem like trivial emails that don't matter. They are not trivial. They do matter.

With a few simple sentences, you can promise you demonstrate that you 1. know how to listen critically, 2. can take direction, 3. can take initiative, and 4. know how to create your own to-do list.

This kind of proactive communication will prove to be one of the most important habits in your career. If I could sum all my good advice up in a single sentence, this would be it: start acting like the dream employee before you ever get the job. Specifically, start *communicating* like the dream employee before you ever get the job.

For confirming the appointment, to be sent the night before or the morning of the interview:

Hi [First Name],
Just confirming our 2pm interview today. I'm looking forward to it.
Thanks!
[Your Name]

For sending a thank-you note, detailing your next steps:

Hi [First Name],

Thank you so much for today's lunch meeting. It was a wonderful help to have you to straighten out my industry terminology, to get some tips on the portfolio, and to get some feedback on how to pitch what I'm trying to do.

Invaluable stuff.

As per our discussion, I am going to get to work on putting together this content marketing portfolio. I've already been doing some research for admirable examples to replicate. I will have something to show you within the next week.

Speak soon,

[Your Name]

Follow through, follow through, follow through.

Before the meeting and after, I specifically call out timeframes. In the confirmation email, I reconfirm the time we're speaking. In the thank-you email, I explicitly lay out what my next steps are and when they should expect to hear from me again.

If someone took 5, 10, 20, 30 minutes out of their day to sit and interview you, or give you some advice, or answer a question, or forward your CV to a colleague, you owe that person an email within 24 hours.

I have spoken to hundreds of powerful people about thank-you notes, because that's just the type of career coach I am. Basic consensus: not every hiring manager seems to think a thank-you note is necessary, but the ones who do care really notice whether or not you send one. If you send one, it might help you. If you don't send one, it might hurt you. Send one.

When interviews and networking meetings go well, you probably already have more stuff to talk about or follow up about later.

Like, in this lunch meeting I reference above. He asked me for a portfolio, so now I owe him a thank you *and* a portfolio.

If you break down the thank-you note example above, I do a few different things:

- I **thank** him for taking the time
- More specifically, I **thank** him for a specific thing we spoke about
- I **reiterate** what he wanted from me (the portfolio)
- I **give a timeline** on when he could expect to see that thing from me

I always sign off an email like this with 'Speak soon' because that's exactly what I want it to be — a segue into the next, and potentially more fruitful, conversation. If there was already an email chain happening, I would write this note back on that same thread. It helps the other person from an organisational perspective *and* you don't have to come up with a new subject line. And it always, always, always, always gets sent within 24 hours of the meeting.

Scheduling and timelines

As we already talked about during the networking lessons, scheduling and next steps are your responsibility if you asked for the meeting or the favour. You set a date and stick to it: 'I'll get you my portfolio by the end of this week. You can expect an email on or before Friday.'

Once you're at the interview stage, the company will set the timelines — but you absolutely deserve to know what will happen next. At the end of an interview (phone or in-person) or in an email, you are totally okay to ask something like: 'I'm definitely interested. When can I expect to hear from you next?'

Checking in and chasing down

What do you do if the day comes and goes when they promised you'd hear back?

Remember that you're the one counting hours and staring at your inbox. Give them a 48-hour grace period — things happen. Remember that they're not on the same timeline as you are. But if they said you'd hear by Tuesday and it's now Thursday afternoon, you are absolutely allowed to follow up.

What if you send over your CV to the contact that asked for it, and you don't hear back?

Give them the benefit of the doubt. Remember that they're doing you a favour. If you send something on a Tuesday and don't hear back for a full week, you're okay to chase them down.

For chasing down an interviewer who hasn't got back to you:

Subject line: *N/A — just hit reply on your most recent email chain*

Hi [Interviewer's Name],

Following up with you here. During my interview, we'd spoken about touching base again this past Tuesday.

I'm still very interested in pursuing the role. If you have any lingering questions before you make this next decision, I'd love to answer them via email or phone.

When do you expect to be making a decision about this next round of interviews? Really looking forward to continuing this process with [Company Name].

Speak soon,

[Your Name]

Interview prep: practice your answer to the 'Tell us about yourself' question

The companies you're dating are also dating other people. They remember why they picked you, but they'll still need a reminder about who you are when you get in the room.

The 'Tell us about yourself' question is not — I repeat, is NOT — a one-size-fits-all answer. Your backstory should be specifically tailored to every situation. The biggest mistake I notice with this question is that people want to go in chronological order, starting from the beginning. As in:

'Well, I'm from Edinburgh originally, and then I got my degree in York. My first internship was ...'

You have to skip over all of that. It may come up in small talk later in the interview, but it's never the right place to start the conversation. If anything, you want to go backwards through your experience, just like with a CV, starting with your most relevant (and usually, most recent and impressive) experience first.

Try this for a template:

- I am a [Desired Job Title] for [Desired Industry].
- I specialise in ... [the three most tangible skills you can bring to the table].
- I love doing these skills because ... [why you are passionate about what you do].
- I am talking to you today because ... [cite the specific kind of value you plan to bring to this business through this position].

Take this example from when I met with a recruiter in the advertising world:

Well, I'm coming at this from the tech world. I've been an independent copywriter for almost five years. I specialise almost exclusively in digital, whether that's optimising words while building an app or directing content strategy for social campaigns. I've never worked inside an agency, and being freelance has given me the chance to experience a lot of projects quite quickly. Now, I'm looking to gauge where I might fit if I decide to pursue a full-time position.

Practise yours in front of the mirror before any interview. Draw inspiration from your LinkedIn summary or cover letter, and remember to always plan it out specifically for that exact situation.

Always remember that this is, after all, a business

A lot of people say they want the job because it's a great learning or growth opportunity. While that's wonderful on a personal level, you know by now that your growth is actually not ideal for the business itself. Very few companies want to pay you to learn. What employers really need is people who know their stuff and, equally as importantly, people who will stay engaged with that work for a considerable length of time.

Whether it's the best company in the world or the worst job you'll ever have, all companies are trying to combat two huge employee-related expenses that you should know about:

1. Apathy: having to pay people who don't want to be there but are doing just enough not to get fired.
2. Turnover: having to spend a lot of time and money to recruit and onboard someone new because the last person who had this job left nine months after they got hired.

What does this mean for you? Instead of highlighting that you want to learn, talk about how interesting the work looks to you. Talk about how the ideas you already have for helping the team to grow and succeed over, say, the next 18–24 months. I literally want you to talk in the interview as if you're going to get hired *and* still be working for the company two years from now.

If you are already asserting from the get-go that you are planning to dig in and engage with your work for the next several months, you stand a much better chance of becoming a long-term asset for the company. And that's what they really need.

Task list: after-the-interview edition

1. Take a few minutes and think through these questions:

    How's your energy level, on a scale from 1 to 10?

    How's your motivation today?

    What was the last job you looked at that really got you excited and hopeful?

It's okay if your answers are '2', 'lower than usual', and 'I can't remember'. This process is hard. It takes a long time to wade through the muck. The important part, as always, is to keep chipping away. And on the days you can't? Take a break. But then get back to it tomorrow.

Final pep talk: let's get you hired

So, that's it. That's all I've learned so far.

You can't keep wasting time waiting for your university degree to be as valuable you were promised it would be (or blaming your career problems on the fact that you don't have a degree). You can't wait for that one person to finally hire you full-time like they said they would, for your boss to give you more responsibility, for someone to tell you what to do with your life. You need to take stock of all your talents, learn why they're useful, find more ways in which you can be useful, ask as many questions as you can, and then — and here's the clincher — come up with your own plan on how you're going to make moves.

Go ahead and rely on yourself. Be clever. Examine your options, and then look one step further to see if that's really the only way to do it. Try your hardest to take what I've given you and keep expanding on it. Slowly but surely, I believe that you will start to see the layers in all things.

Should finding a job be this hard? Definitely not. Capitalism is wild.

But you and I both know that the world spins madly on whether you make your move or you don't. Waiting for someone else to swoop in and save the day, historically, never seems to work out very well for anybody. This is what it is to be an #ENTRYLEVELBOSS, dear friend. You have to be the CEO of your own career. You need to do it now. No one else on earth can do that job except for you.

Keep growing. Keep building your skillset. Keep becoming excellent.

And I know you will, because ... you've got this. Yes, you have.

We don't all fit in this nice, neat little box when it comes to our careers. You are going to have to be unafraid to fight for what you want, and be able to eloquently prove that you are the best person for this job. And while that's time-consuming and emotionally exhausting, it's also kind of great. Maybe — just maybe — it means all the power is in your hands.

Are you still going to run into incompetent people who let you down? Yup. Will it happen more than once? Probably. Are you going to talk to managers who don't seem to get why you are so clearly meant for this role? For sure. But you didn't want to work for them anyway, remember?

In the end, it all comes down to a single idea you need to keep at the back of your head, a thought you can return to every time you feel like giving up and hiding under the rug:

They need you. They need you so, so, so, so much more than you need them.

Work hard.

Be confident.

Be interesting and, more importantly, *interested.*

Be unafraid to provide solutions to your employer's problems.

You've got this. And I cannot wait to see how it all works out. Please email me at heyalexa@entrylevelboss.com and tell me all about it.

Big love,

Alexa

Bonus chapter: Emails from my personal archive

I really, really, really want to make sure you can spot the word-for-word differences between an email that could change your life and one that looks like a missed opportunity — and I am prepared to publicly shame myself in order to do it.

Back when I was at university, I created a purple Gmail folder which I appropriately titled 'Job Search Stuff'. I dutifully stored all of my professional correspondence in there for the first several years of my career. So many unanswered job applications, so many hopes and dreams from my past.

Good, bad, and ugly — these four emails all come directly from that folder. I was not always good at this. I made my own fair share of failed attempts to break into the professional world, and you're about to read some of them.

If you feel called out or personally attacked while reading some of these 'bad' emails, take comfort in knowing just how many of us are right there with you. Plus, the moment you bought this book, you started putting in the work to level up your career and your communication style, so … #growth.

Email #1: Lousy

Subject line: *Application submission*

Mr X and Mr Y,

Attached are the three required documents for [Company Name]'s management trainee application. Thank you so much for this opportunity.

What a missed opportunity. What I vaguely remember about this job application was that there were very detailed directions laid out on the website. They told me to put together three documents — a cover letter, writing sample, and CV — and then email those attachments to two people.

When I sent this email, I'm sure I thought to myself, 'Well done me. This email looks very professional and I gave them exactly what they wanted. They'll probably call me tomorrow.' Yeah, I never heard from them.

You need to constantly consider the experience for the person on the receiving end of your emails. It is someone's job to read through a stack of applications. They are literally assigned to sit there and look for you. How can you create a more joyful experience for that person? How can you brighten their day? With each interaction: be a human, speaking to a human.

In this email, I don't address these two as if they're real humans. I don't introduce myself, I use strange words (see: 'Attached are the required documents …'), and I don't make any effort to be personable. I certainly don't make it seem like I want the job. The whole exchange, left in my hands, feels sad and transactional.

This was my first impression moment and I screwed it up. I missed the opportunity to build rapport and show these employers just how much warmth and enthusiasm they could expect from a candidate like me. No wonder I never heard anything back.

Email #2: Still lousy

Subject line: *Recruitment inquiry*

[Company Name]!

I obtained this contact information via the [Company Name] website and am writing to inquire about any available lower-level positions within your company that might be available and suitable for my unique skillset.

Attached is my CV for your perusal. Thank you so much for your time and consideration; I look forward to hearing back from you soon.

All my best,

Alexa Shoen

What is up with this subject line? Am I a recruiter? Do I want to hire them? What was I thinking? If I were to see this subject line in my own inbox from someone who was trying to get a job with #ENTRYLEVELBOSS, I'd think it was robot spam from some lousy company trying to sell me a service to … help me recruit people …?

Taught myself everything I know, folks, taught myself everything I know.

I went through a period of time where I really wanted to work for an advertising agency. I spent weeks on this self-inflicted research project where I looked up every single advertising agency I could find in my target market(s) of San Francisco, LA, New York, London, and Paris. (Five, by the way, is too many target markets.) I wasn't concerned about the specifics of any of these agencies, I was just hell-bent on finding email addresses. The more the better. Without doing any real research about any of these companies, I copy-and-pasted some version of this blurb to hundreds of info@ agencyiknewnothingabout.com email addresses. And I do mean hundreds. It was a well-intentioned initiative, but not a well exe-cuted one.

Let's break it down.

'I obtained this contact information ...'

This first line comes straight from a cover letter template I'd been given at university. I was trying to give context for why I was get-ting in touch, but I completely blew it. Why so formal? Why so awkward? I was taking it way too seriously without being at all strategic. I was using strange 'professional person' language that didn't even sound like me.

I should have introduced myself in plain English and said I was looking for an internship or a shot at an entry-level position. I should have asked if they had a graduate scheme. I should have researched what kinds of roles exist within a normal agency, so that I could speak articulately about the differences between a copy-writer, an account manager, and a production coordinator. The key mistake, above all else, was that I tried to put all the responsibility onto the reader. I was asking them to tell me what kind of job I should have, based on 'my unique skillset'.

I see this mistake pretty frequently. I have warned you about this mistake at least once already. *Here I am! Here's me! This is my CV. I typed it up myself. Here you go. Will you, person I just met, please scan your entire company structure and look for holes that you might be able to plug with my unique skillset?*

You need to put in the work. While we can never truly know how a company's teams and departments are organised by peer-ing in from the outside, we can make educated guesses. This skill gets sharper over time as you see the inner workings of more and more businesses. It's never a good idea to say to somebody, 'Here are my seventeen talents. I'm not sure if they're helpful. Are they helpful? Please go find a position inside your company that's right for me.'

TIP

In a cold email like this one, try linking the person to the online job posting most similar to what you're looking for, even if it's a posting from a different company. Do whatever you can to specifically illustrate what kind of job you're looking for (and *right* for), so that the recipient can quickly map you to their own company organisational chart. It's okay to ask for exactly what you want. You're not being presumptuous, you're being *helpful*.

If I had done my homework, just look at what I could've said in this email:

- 'I want to intern for your social media team.'
- 'Do you ever hire new grads for the production team? I want to help you.'
- 'This is my portfolio. I want to be your new junior social media copywriter.'

Put a title to what it is that you're looking for, even if you've never had that title before. Learn to use the language of your opponent so that you can speak your new reality into existence. Study until you are able to wield those words like a finely sculpted sword. No one — not your favourite cousin, not your cool neighbour — is going to take 15–20 minutes out of their own work day to try to find a spot for your skills, then chase down the right hiring manager for you in a building down the road, and then take even more time to teach you what that role would require. Always refocus on bringing a solution to the table for the employer, instead of shouting into the void about your own unemployment problem.

Email #3: Getting better

Subject line: *New bright-eyed Domer in San Francisco*

Hi First Name,

I'm Alexa: Notre Dame class of 2011 graduate, and a recent transplant to San Francisco. After finishing my MA in England earlier this year, I've set up shop on American soil again. As I learn more about San Francisco's vibrant advertising industry — which I am passionately and earnestly attempting to break into — I've come across [Company Name]'s work multiple times. You can imagine my delight upon realising it was headed up by one of our own.

If you have any time for a young alumna, I would very much so appreciate your advice and expertise on getting through the door and into the (big b)ad world. In particular, I'd love to chat with your creative services team about my copywriting and brand strategy aspirations.

I'd love to buy you a pint or a coffee, or chat with you on the phone. Thanks so much for taking the time to read through my eager request — I'll look forward to hearing from you soon.

Best,

Alexa

This is an email that I sent to an alumni contact when I desperately needed a new job in San Francisco. After finding (or guessing) accurate work email addresses for all the alumni in the Bay Area who were working in my desired industry, I crafted an email for each and every person. Of the 5–8 emails I sent, 100% of people replied — which is pretty impressive considering that they were all strangers to me. There's a reason why I keep repeating myself about the silly but human act of establishing common ground when you first meet somebody. The small-talk techniques that feel dull at birthday parties are suddenly the reason someone decides to return your email. See:

Me: Where are you from?
You: Newport!
Me: Oh, no way! My aunt lives in Newport!
You: Oh, cool! What part of town?

You don't need to be a carbon copy of the hiring manager. You don't need to be 'one of them', whatever that means in your world. It's okay if you grew up differently, if you don't have the right pedigree, if you don't think you're the 'kind' of person who gets the good jobs or gets to talk to the fancy people. At the end of the day, it all comes down to this: humans just want to hire competent, friendly people they trust. Your job is not to pretend to be somebody else. Your job is to be the most highly skilled version of yourself, to reach out, to make some small talk, and to break the ice.

University alumni — or, if you didn't go to university, people who went to the same secondary school as you — are a great group of people to practise Magical Spark networking on. Even if you never would have been friends with this person had you been the same age, they are pretty likely to respond to your emails — because we all have those foundational memories from our teens and early twenties. A lot of those memories are related to where we attended school or university.

Again, let's break it down.

'New bright-eyed Domer in San Francisco'

I put two key pieces of information directly into the subject line:

1. I call out that it's an alumni connection immediately by referring to myself as a **Domer**, the nickname for students who attended the University of Notre Dame.
2. I announce that I'm **new to San Francisco**, so physically located in the same city as this person.

He hasn't even opened the email yet and I've already established a tribal bond which he can interpret as: *Hey, I'm new around here. I basically just graduated. I don't know what's going on. This is all really hard. Throw me a bone here — I'm trying.*

'*I'm Alexa: Notre Dame, class of 2011 graduate and a recent transplant ...*'

Finally, an email where I introduce myself! Folks, this book is only so many pages long, and I won't have many more times to underscore just how important this technique is for your career success. A solid introduction might as well be the foundational secret sauce of becoming an #ENTRYLEVELBOSS, come to think of it.

'*You can imagine my delight upon realising it was headed up by one of our own.*'

I do not know this person. We are not friends. I'm ... flirting in good faith. It's a bit cheeky, but not disrespectful.

'*If you have any time for a young alumna ...*'

I'm backtracking from the bravado of 'one of our own', and acknowledging that we're not equals in this game. *You're wise, and I don't know what I'm doing. Please help.*

'*In particular, I'd love to chat with your creative services team about my copywriting and brand strategy aspirations.*'

Even though I had no idea what I was doing or how to get in the door, I made the effort to get really specific about what I wanted. I went beyond just asking for 'some time to pick your brain about this kind of career path'.

If memory serves me correctly, the recipient of this email was the chief financial officer (CFO) of the advertising agency, who was a good 30 years older than me. I didn't waste his time by pretending I cared about finance. I said, 'If I can chat with you, great. But if I can chat with these people you could introduce me to, even better. That's where my career is headed.'

Always dig one level deeper and ask for exactly what you want. Even if you're not 100% sure that this is your life direction forever (and who *is* sure?), you're at least proving to the recipient that you've done your homework. If you know what this person can do to help you, tell them.

'*... my eager request*'

I know, but I warned you! I don't know what I'm really talking about. Please help me anyway.

'*I'll look forward to hearing from you soon.*'

I leave with my head held high. *I know I'm young, I know I took a shot, and I'm trying to be as confident I can be. Here's hoping that my bravery will be rewarded with a response.*

What I could have done better: I specifically mention that I want to talk to the creative services team, but then I go vague at the end by just asking him if he's up for a chat. In this case, it turned out well for me. If the connection had been looser (a total stranger instead of an alumni contact), I probably would have been more explicit about exactly what I wanted.

If I had been more senior: This email would not have highlighted my skillset strongly enough. If you are starting to become an expert at something (or have already been an expert for years), you need to play those cards from the start and lay out what you can offer.

Result: I had an email back from this person that very same day, and interviewed with his company the next week. Not half-bad for a total stranger.

Email #4: Pretty good

Subject line: *New community manager in Berlin*

Hey [First Name] —

Hope this email finds you well! I'm Alexa. I've been following [Company Name] and the Berlin tech scene for the last few months, as I'm moving to your fabulous city in two weeks!

I'm coming to Berlin from Silicon Valley, where I've been working in content strategy and community management for a Crunchie-nominated, venture-backed online education startup. [My Employer] specialises in photo education, so I have a true soft spot for what [Company Name] is doing.

I wanted to reach out to you now, as I'm sure you're incredibly busy, and see if I could buy you lunch/coffee/beer and talk shop about community management, maybe pick your brain on the Berlin startup world.

Are you in town the 7–10 of May? Let me know what you think.

Cheers!

Have a lovely night,

Alexa

Here I was doing the work (again) to create a network out of thin air in a new city: Berlin. Didn't have a job lined up, had never visited, was moving there anyways. Go me.

This email was written for a peer, and it's a great example of why you shouldn't aim straight for the top of the food chain. This woman had graduated from university a year before me. She was doing a job very similar to the job I'd been doing in San Francisco for the last few months. She was, you might say, the right fit for me.

Your peers might not have a ton of power yet, but they do have time. A CEO won't have more than 10 minutes to give you on the phone, and you'd better know exactly what you want to ask for during that call. The junior editorial assistant, on the other hand, will be surprised and flattered to get your email. Her inbox will be less noisy. She will remember what it's like to be in your shoes. She may have been in your shoes just a few months earlier. And here you come, making her feel like she made it. Like she's important. And she is important — to you!

Networking with people your own age is where it's at, friend. By developing connections with peers in your own industry, you are building a web of people who will be right by your side as you all grow up and climb the professional ranks together. I can think of no better long-term career success strategy.

'New community manager in Berlin'

For the subject line, I'm using the same tactic I used in the last email. Here's who I am, here's where I am, here's why you should care.

'... as I'm moving to your fabulous city in two weeks!'

I introduce myself super quickly. *Hi, I'm stalking you a little bit, but I promise to not be annoying or weird about it. This is a networking email. I'm reaching out in good faith.*

Never underestimate just how short someone's attention span will be for this email. They're deciding within two sentences as to whether or not they're going to keep reading. Provide context quickly. Get to the ask.

The second paragraph: I make my pitch

By this point in my career, only I had about a year's worth of work experience under my belt, but I knew enough to know how to speak industry lingo and pitch my own skillset. In this second paragraph, I'm setting up my shot. I'm providing context as to who I am and, much more importantly, indirectly, why it might affect you.

Terms like 'Crunchie-nominated' and 'venture-backed' signal that I was working for a hot tech startup, even if the reader had never heard of them. The underlined phrase linked to a high-profile press piece about the company, to provide additional context without spending the additional word count. Frankly, I wanted to highlight that we are equals. *Hey look, I made your job easy — I came and found you. I would be a great hire!*

The third paragraph: I make my ask

I get as specific as I can, considering this is a relatively junior employee and a total stranger. *Hey, meet with me. Let's see if this makes sense. I think your boss should hire me.*

    'Are you in town the 7–10 of May?'

Don't make someone look through their calendar and ask *you* when *you're* free. Remember that it's always your responsibility to propose the time.

Epilogue: This girl was super rad. She responded, I went to her office, and we talked about photography and California. And then I ended up going out for a BBQ with all of her friends/colleagues, some of whom I still hang out with from time to time. This is also the company that didn't hire me because of the 37% Rule (see page 32), but I'd still send this email in a heartbeat if given the chance.

Unanswered emails, rejection, and the game of marketing
Networking means going into the business of marketing yourself. Job searching in general, as you've likely gleaned by now, means going into the business of marketing yourself. I want you to manage your expectations about how many people will respond to the emails you send out.

The art of marketing pretty much always operates on the concept of a funnel. You start with a lot of people (funnels are wide at the top) in order to ultimately end up with a handful of paying customers (funnels are super skinny at the bottom).

To illustrate, let's say a business boasts 12 million newsletter subscribers. That sounds like an insanely big number — but that's just the first step. Statistically speaking, you can expect 15% of those 12 million people to ever even open the email, and that's on a really good day. That immediately shrinks your 'real' number down to 1.8 million people. Many of those 1.8 million people only open the email in order to delete it. For a newsletter of any shape or size, you can optimistically expect about 1.5% of the original 12 million people to respond, click on a button, or do whatever it was you wanted them to do. And so the number shrinks again. From 12 million people down to 180,000 people. You started out with a population the size of Paris and wound up with a group the size of Mobile, Alabama.

Marketers prepare for this. That's why they send out the *best possible content* they can to *the highest number of people*. The better job they do at approaching their potential customer base, the more likely they are to see that important 180,000 number grow slowly over time.

Thinking about the funnel is now your job, too.

Your mission is to send out *the best possible content* to *the highest number of people*. Most people only play the numbers game (see: spamming your CV to any recruiters or hiring managers you can find) without doing the best possible content part. You must send *good* content to the *right* people. You are not guaranteed a response — but if you do the best you can, and you keep trying, and keep improving the way you approach people, you are going to get yourself some customers. You can't possibly know if someone saw your message or not. You can't possibly know why they did or did not respond. All you can control is the practice of sending out great emails to the right people.

Don't get caught pinning your hopes on one single person. Reframe the unanswered emails and messages as a natural part of the process. You may find the perfect person to email or tweet at, and then they'll still drop the ball or stop responding to your messages. Keep going. You are so much further ahead than almost anybody else. You are actually trying.

All you need is that one **YES!** that will turn your world upside down.

A thank-you gift from me

Reader, thank you so much for taking the time to read this book. You're the coolest. If I've helped you to reframe your job search and your approach to career growth, even in some small way, I'm honestly delighted.

Now, importantly, I want to talk to you about how we can stay in touch.

First, join my free mailing list. I send a weekly-ish newsletter to thousands of job seekers like you, talking about my approach to my own career and answering questions from readers. If you liked this book, you'll love my emails.

Subscribe at: **alexashoen.com/join-now/**

I'd also like to offer you a free gift. How about we go through this whole job search process together? We can. In fact, that's my job. Any reader of this book is entitled to a 20% discount on the enrolment fee for #ELB School, my magical job search boot camp that expands on the 9-step method you just learned about in this book. You don't have to do this alone.

To claim your discount (valued at £99), go to:

entrylevelboss.com/thankyoureader

Acknowledgements

I had absolutely no idea what I was getting myself into when I agreed to a meeting with Jessica Killingley. I'd always thought that #ENTRYLEVELBOSS would make for a decent book someday, but you were the first one to say, 'No, you've *really* got something here. Go write me a proposal.' Thank you for your snark, your support, and your guidance. You were right: books change lives.

To Jason Bartholomew and James Spackman: working with The BKS Agency has been a joy from Day 1. Thank you for the wisdom and the banter.

To Laura Apperson, my first editor at St Martin's Press: your acquisition turned my world upside down. Thank you for believing in this book and for continuing to advise me long after you were contractually obligated to do so.

To Hannah Braaten and Nettie Finn at St Martin's Press: you elegantly picked this book up and ran with it. Thank you for your encouragement, flexibility, and humour.

To Molly Slight and Sarah Braybrooke at Scribe Publications: you pushed me to make this book as strong as it possibly could be and I admire you so freaking much for that. Thank you.

To Gemma Milne: thank you for being my book wife. Every author should be so lucky as to go through their first traditional publishing deal with such a dear friend.

To Dr Christian Busch: your workshop at the 2019 Sandbox London Retreat helped me to drastically reframe the networking chapters in Part 3 of this book. If that isn't serendipity, I don't know what is.

To my former co-workers at Facebook: thank you for cheering me on and for allowing me to resign so gracefully in order to go write this manuscript. And thank you for reminding me that I'd always be welcome back someday, too.

To every early reader who read through my giant Google doc: you pointed out the plot holes, you forced me to reflect on my assumptions, you highlighted the sentences that made you smile. Thank you. I'd especially like to call out Ange Royall-Kahin, Cailey Ryckman, Shanna Gast, Danae Shell, and Sally Lloyd for their brilliant feedback.

To Teshia Treuhaft: this book, and especially the original book proposal, would simply not have been made possible without your sofa. Thank you. I love you.

To Chelsea Milojkovic: you are my chosen sister in this life. Thank you. I love you.

To David Riaño Molina and Ed Bentley: the three of us somehow managed to bring an incredibly dope album into the world in parallel to me writing this book (seriously, everybody, go look me up on Spotify). I am so grateful for both of you.

To my family: #ENTRYLEVELBOSS simply does not exist without you. Dad, this book is filled with as much of your pragmatic advice as it is with mine. Mom, this book is filled with as much of your emotional intelligence and encouragement as it is with mine. Meegs, you believe in me on the days when I don't believe in myself. I love you all so much. Thank you.

Thank you to every single person who ever heard about this book and said, 'That sounds like a really good idea.' Thank you to every single person who sent me job search stories. And, oh man, thank you to every single friend who bought me lunch, took me out, DM'd me words of encouragement, or offered me a place to crash anytime during 2019. How grateful I am to have surrounded myself with such a motley crew of geniuses in this life.

Most importantly, thank you to all the people who trusted me to give out #ENTRYLEVELBOSS advice long before this book ever came out. To every single one of my students, to every person who ever emailed me with a question: you are incredible. I hope I've done you justice in these pages. I am rooting for you, always.

About the Author

Alexa Shoen, born in 1989, is the internet's leading confidant for panicking job seekers and the CEO of #ENTRYLEVELBOSS: an online education company that transforms those job seekers into hired, happy professionals. She previously worked in design for Facebook, leading cross-platform initiatives to optimise the company's multi-billion-dollar advertising business. Before that, she was one of the most sought-after communication consultants in the European tech industry and advised high-growth companies in Berlin, London, and New York. Alexa is a beneficiary of the UK's Exceptional Talent (Technology) visa scheme, a prestigious immigration route awarded to just 200 world-leading technologists annually. She's also an acclaimed independent jazz vocalist. Alexa is originally from San Diego, California.